then & **Plymouth** now

written & compiled by
Chris Robinson

edited by
Ben Robinson

pen&ink
PUBLISHING

British Library Cataloguing in Publication Data
Robinson Chris 1954 –
Plymouth Then & Now, photographic comparisons 1860s - 2004
1.Devon. Plymouth, history
1. Title
942.3'58

ISBN 09543 4801 X

Designed By Chris Robinson
Cover design by Ewan McKnight
Edited by Ben Robinson
© Chris Robinson 2004

First published October 2004

OTHER CHRIS ROBINSON TITLES
PUBLISHED BY PEN & INK

PLYMOUTH AS TIME DRAWS ON – 1985
PLYMOUTH AS TIME DRAWS ON VOL 2 – 1988
VICTORIAN PLYMOUTH: AS TIME DRAWS ON – 1991
PUBS OF PLYMOUTH PAST AND PRESENT
The Harvest Home and one hundred others – 1995
PUBS OF PLYMOUTH PAST AND PRESENT
Prince George and one hundred others – 1997
UNION STREET – 2000
THE ARGYLE BOOK – 2002
ELIZABETHAN PLYMOUTH – 2002

Published by
Pen & Ink Publishing
34 New Street
Barbican
Plymouth PL1 2NA
tel; 01752 705337/228120
fax; 01752 770001
www.chrisrobinson.co.uk

Printed & bound in Great Britain by
Latimer Trend & Company Ltd
Estover Close
Plymouth PL6 7PL
Devon

then & Plymouth now

Introduction

There will be many who, having looked at the title of this book and then the images on the cover, will have thought to themselves ... "That's not Now!" But then ask yourself "When is Now?" As soon as the question has been aired it's a part of the past. All moments pass - all things must pass - nothing lasts forever. And that is precisely why, rather than run around town and bring all the new images up to date, I thought it would be better to just record the date that the piece was first published in the Herald ... and leave it at that. Although, just for the hell of it I did go and photograph the site of the new Drake Circus development this morning so that at least, for Now, the book does have an up to date version of the cover scene. But how long will it look like that, and how long after the development is finally finished will that eventually last? We have no idea of knowing, we can only guess. And for the record, my guess is that it probably won't last as long as the ill-fated 1970s Drake Circus development. Time will tell.

Drake Circus - 7 November 2004

In the meantime, as you work your way through the words and pictures of this volume, I guarantee that on more than one occasion you will laugh out loud at some innocent remark that has already been rendered ridiculous by the passing of the months and years since it first appeared. "C'est la vie," say the old folk, "It goes to show you never can tell" ... as that wonderful Rock'n'Roll poet Charles Berry, better known as Chuck, once said.

And so here you have it, a contemporary look at the ever-changing face of the City. Clearly, in Plymouth's case, wholesale changes were precipitated by the aerial bombardment sustained during World War II. Seventy-two acres of prime City Centre land was compulsorily purchased, flattened and redeveloped, all largely according to the prescription laid down in that inspirational and visionary 1943 Plan for Plymouth drawn up by the City's Engineer, James Paton Watson, and the greatly revered Town Planner, Patrick Abercrombie. Even now, over sixty years on, that Plan is never far from the minds of those involved in shaping the future of the City and its very existence has almost certainly been the reason that so many others have sought to produce subsequent Plans for Plymouth. I worked a little bit on one - Tomorrow's Plymouth - with City Planner, Chris Shepley, nearly twenty years ago, although undoubtedly the most notable is the blueprint recently produced at the City's request by another internationally renowned architectural planner, David Mackay.

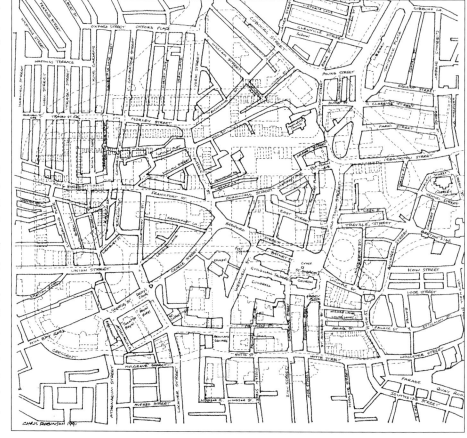

Happily however, this time the wish list has not been produced in the wake of the large scale destruction and devastation of the fabric of the city; rather the Mackay Vision has been produced to try and prevent any crass commercial desecration of the soul of the City and to try and steer future development in a direction worthy of Paton Watson and Abercrombie - and worthy of a 'City of the World'.

Whatever does happen over the next five to ten years one thing is absolutely certain; the landscape will change here and there. Indeed look around the City now and you will see that it is already happening on a scale not witnessed here since the 1950s. As a small army of tall cranes break cover, piercing the skyline all around the town, it seems that Plymouth, at last, is going up in the world. With Argyle, Albion and the Raiders all climbing higher than they have been for years - if not ever - it seems inevitable too that the buildings are going to get higher, and higher, as they have been in other cities for many, many years.

It's a change that not all will welcome, but the tide is unlikely to turn now. There will be plenty of changes to record and, already, many are they in this age of digital imagery who have already been out with their cameras and camcorders, watching workmen, documenting diggers and filming foundations – just as many did with more rudimentary equipment fifty years ago.

As for me, I've just been doing it for the last twenty years. Plenty long enough to know that producing a book like this is like writing a story that has no ending - and no real middle or beginning either. So it is that this modest volume simply sets out to take you on a virtual walking tour of the heart of the City. We start with a good look at Plymouth's finest asset, the 'jewel in the crown,' Plymouth Hoe. What other cities can boast such a fine public open space with such spectacular views - so little changed over the years?

Then we wander down and around the old part of town, that part that was seemingly of so little consequence during the last war that the Luftwaffe largely ignored it, leaving great chunks of the Elizabethan town intact for the planners to pull down *after* the war. Believe it or not more precious old buildings were demolished in the fifties than were destroyed during the Blitz. Were it not for that noble group of conservationists that came together as the Barbican Association in the mid-fifties, the fine four-hundred-year-old building that has housed my shop and gallery in New Street for over twenty years would have been bulldozed half a century ago along with dozens of other treasured gems.

And then we're in the City Centre; mixing old images of pre and post-war Plymouth, we end up with that section of the tour that more than any other is part-nostalgia, part-history. As links with the pre-war City become increasingly thin on the ground in the modern shopping centre, our pictorial pairings range from delightfully simple Spot the Difference affairs to the brain teasing, Does X Really Mark the Spot? To help with the latter, I've included a couple of overlaid maps I drew up a few years ago to better relate the old to the new. I hope you have as much fun looking at them, and the pictures, as I did making them and taking them – the Now photographs that is … although, actually, some of the not-so-old Then pictures are mine too – where does the time go?

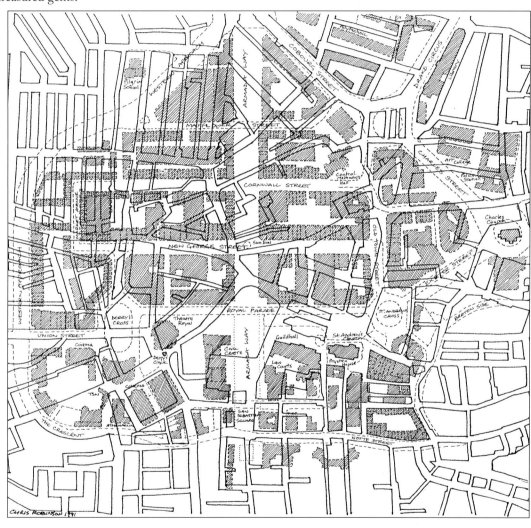

Chris Robinson
November 2004

Twenty years separate these two images and in that time the fresh-faced young artist and author in our Then photograph has gone on to produce hundreds of drawings and hundreds of thousands of words about the City. Maintaining his base in New Street now since 1978, few know the City as well and no-one has written more about it.

ACKNOWLEDGEMENTS

Regular readers of the Evening Herald will probably be familiar with much of this material. Produced over an eight year period, almost all of these Then and Nows have been featured in the 'Looking Back' pages that appear every Saturday. Some have formed the backbone of various Herald supplements, but never before have they been brought together in such a large collection and in such a logical order.

It is our hope that you will find it fascinating, and informative, although it does not aspire to being a particularly heavy, academic, slice of local history.

I am indebted to the Herald for providing the rationale for this – and most of the other books I've written on Plymouth. I started producing the Saturday 'As Time Draws On' feature for them back in February 1982 and haven't missed a week since then! The various articles and pictures have been reworked into half a dozen tomes already and there are plenty more in the pipeline.

So thanks specifically to Alan Qualtrough, the paper's editor, and to the features team, Mike Bramall, Martin Freeman and Katie Tokus. Thanks, too, to Pete Holgate and generations of Herald and Morning News photographers who have inadvertently provided many of the Then images. More specifically thanks to local photographers Roy Westlake, Roy Todd, Doug Flood, Peter Waterhouse, the late Frank Osborne and any others who have kindly provided images over the years. Thanks too to Terry Guswell, Duncan Godefroy, Winifred Hooper, Sylvia Boulden, Joan Dancer, and countless Herald readers who have furnished me with fine old photos from their own archives – and to the City Museum and Art Gallery, the Local Studies Library and various picture postcard firms of yesteryear.

With so many photographs coming from so many sources – and with so little information, if anything at all, ever recorded on the back of them, it is impossible to credit everyone. I know, though, how infuriating it is to find your work being used with no credit so may I therefore apologise in advance to anyone who feels neglected in this respect. The publishers would be happy to hear from anyone who has information concerning the copyright of any un-credited images.

On a practical note, thanks to Doreen Mole for archiving all these articles and photographs and thanks to Ben Robinson for sorting through piles of computer files and pulling all the saved texts and pictures together and arranging them in a logical sequence. On the proof-reading front thanks to the outlaws, Patricia and Laurie Greathead, Rob Warren and the lovely Clare, my publisher, who's as wonderful Now as she was Then.

On the design and production front, enormous thanks to Ewan McKnight for his ideas and even temper and on the printing and production front thanks to all at Latimer Trend, especially Bob Mills whose support and back up has always been absolutely first-class.

Contents

then & now Plymouth

written & compiled by
Chris Robinson

PLYMOUTH HOE FROM THE AIR Then, Then and Now ... Our earliest aerial snap takes us back to May 1938, when the pier, rather than Smeaton's Tower, was perhaps the Hoe's most prominent feature. Not too far behind them both was the Bandstand, seen here to the left of the lighthouse, the large ring around it indicating the usual extent of the seating for major concerts. Note how the bathing facilities at Tinside had been fully developed but the changing facilities and the walkway above, features that the post war generation are most familiar with, had not yet taken shape. Note, too, how, in the middle picture, from 1985, how the old Mallard Café had appeared in that former wild space beneath the little octagonal lookout building above Tinside and how just a few years later it was replaced by the Dome which now occupies even more of that site.

PIER GROUPS There's every chance that the group pictured here on the grass had either just been on the Pier or were about to take a stroll around it. One of the first public structures in the Three Towns to be 'lighted by electricity', the Pier was opened in the late 1870s, but, on account of financial constraints, not fully completed until 1891, when a 2,000 seater pavilion was created on the end of it. Even then the original plans were still left a little unfulfilled, as the idea had been to create an extra stretch of promenade to take strollers back up over the road right into the bull ring. The town turned that idea down and by the time the pavilion had been built, the local authorities had created the multi-layered, colonnaded Belvedere that we see here, set like a wedding cake into the Hoe slopes. It's a structure that, like Smeaton's Tower too, looks as fine today as it did then, unlike the Pier, a victim of the Blitz in 1941.

WEST HOE BATHS Apart from the Pier it's a view that hasn't changed all that much since that great tourist icon, Smeaton's Tower arrived on the Hoe slopes back in 1882. Prior to the 1880s - the decade that formal gardens and statuary were first imposed on the Hoe - this was an altogether more rugged area, epitomised by the sea-assaulted and weather-beaten rocks we see here in the foreground. It was here, incidentally, at West Hoe that local bathers were first able to swim without necessarily having to brave the waves. The structure we see in the foreground on the right having been created as the West Hoe Baths long before the development of Tinside.

THE BELVEDERE "There are few more pleasant methods of spending a spare hour than by taking a saunter on the Hoe on a fine summer afternoon ... the liveliness of the scene caused by the assemblage of hundreds of persons of both sexes and from amongst the most fashionable classes of society; the gay dresses of the ladies, who here delight to display all the adornments which nature and fashion combined, have bestowed upon them." The quote is from a local guide book of 1879, predating our Then picture by some years and proving that, just as the pictures suggest, some things simply don't change all that much.

PLYMOUTH PIER   For anyone unfamiliar with contemporary dinghies, the small craft used in the foreground look much the same as those used today. The tall ships in the distance, however, are seldom seen these days.   The difference between the two images is around 100 years, and if you look carefully you can see that Drake's Island in our Then picture looks far more of a military base and less rural than it does now. Otherwise Mount Edgecumbe looks much the same today, as does the corner of Grand Parade. But the most striking contrast between the two pictures is Plymouth Pier ... and the absence of it now.   Reduced to a burnt-out skeleton of twisted metal in the Blitz of March 1941, all that remains is a short section of hardstanding that the pleasure boats use to load and off load their passengers.   Happily, we have a large number of postcards and photographs to remind us of those 50 odd years when Plymouth had a pier, and the heady days in the late 1930s when the pier and the lido were open on the Hoe. *EH 27 Nov 1999*

WEST HOE More than a century separates these two images of West Hoe, but there are more similarities than differences. However, the differences we see speak volumes about the changes in the way we live. Structurally, it is the absence of the pier, the additions to Grand Parade and the little cluster that currently houses the Wet Wok Chinese restaurant that indicates the passage of time. But look at the Sound. A century ago, there were a couple of dozen boats of various shapes and sizes, moored or in action in this scene. Then there were three tall ships anchored off Drake's Island and two paddle steamers alongside the little harbour at West Hoe. Today there is one white-sailed dinghy in the distance, as road and air travel has largely superseded seagoing traffic, and where there were few pedestrians strolling along the pavement we now see dozens of cars. *EH 23 Sept 2000*

LEIGHAM STREET These were some of the most delightfully located residences in Plymouth. With the old quarry at West Hoe across Cliff Road in front of them, there was nothing to obscure their panoramic view of the Sound and the greenery of Mount Edgcumbe and Jennycliff on either side of it. It was known simply as the Terrace – and if you were going to live in any terrace in Plymouth this would have surely been one of the most desirable. It stood at the bottom of Leigham Street, an area that was quite badly bombed in the early part of the war. Some years after the war the site was cleared and today the Forte Post House (the former Mayflower Hotel) stands on this site. *EH 05 May 1998*

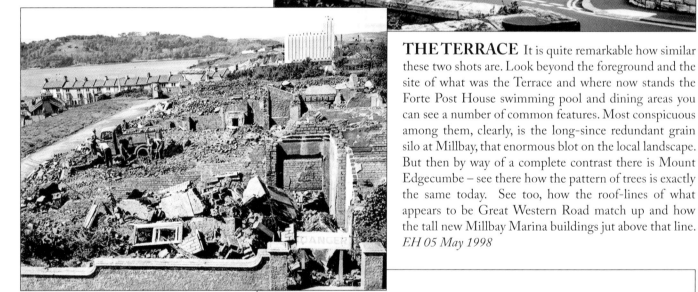

THE TERRACE It is quite remarkable how similar these two shots are. Look beyond the foreground and the site of what was the Terrace and where now stands the Forte Post House swimming pool and dining areas you can see a number of common features. Most conspicuous among them, clearly, is the long-since redundant grain silo at Millbay, that enormous blot on the local landscape. But then by way of a complete contrast there is Mount Edgcumbe – see there how the pattern of trees is exactly the same today. See too, how the roof-lines of what appears to be Great Western Road match up and how the tall new Millbay Marina buildings jut above that line. *EH 05 May 1998*

THE HOE LOOKING WEST There are pre-war pictures of Plymouth Hoe from many angles, but few show this view. We see the old Royal Western Yacht Club, the top of Leigham Street and the quarrymen's cottages across the top of West Hoe where the Mayflower Hotel currently stands. It is unusual to see any pre-war view without either the pier (although we see the entrance) or Smeaton's Tower. It is remarkable how much of the view has remained unchanged. *EH 06 March 2004*

THE HOE FROM THE SEA How many differences can you spot? Ignoring the obvious – like the passing presence of the fair and the big wheel – they are few and far between. Only when you get over to the far righthand side of the pictures and see that the Mallard Café has given way to the Plymouth Dome is there any clear clue to the date of the earlier image. It's comfortably post 1965, because that's when the Café opened and because Smeaton's Tower is striped, as it was on the Eddystone but not always on the Hoe (the red bands were re-instated largely thanks to Peter Stedman who was then a leading light of the Plymouth Chamber of Commerce), and pre-1988 because of the Dome, but how much more precisely can you place it?

HOE FORESHORE While change on the Hoe has been slow and subtle over the last hundred years, there is always something to warrant a second look. Here we see a view of the top of Smeaton's Tower in 1892 – just 10 years after it arrived on the green slopes of the Hoe. The view appears to have been taken from the pier and is difficult to duplicate exactly today. You can see just how different the vantage point is by looking at the difference in distances between the top of the tower and the octagonal observation tower in the two pictures. Clearly, the most striking differences, though, are in the covered colonnade that accompanied the development of the Tinside lido in the 1920s and 1930s; and the construction of the Plymouth Dome in the late 1980s. *EH 10 June 2000*

TINSIDE If you've ever wondered what Tinside looked like before they started creating concrete bathing facilities here on the waterfront, then take a good look at this wonderful old photograph taken by Winifred Hooper's father in 1891. Standing proud on the beach is the 'Man Rock' that unfortunately was a victim of the development here. The area was already popular with bathers and it is interesting to note that there is already development in place at the back of the Lido site just below the Pier. *EH Dec 2004*

TINSIDE Doubtless, in years to come, the period of closure that separates these two images will be forgotten and, hopefully, the young generation that has recently been allowed to, once more, discover the joys of Tinside, will do their bit to ensure that the future of this wonderful facility is never again dictated by simplistic financial considerations. As a piece of architecture, a slice of heritage and source of pleasure this is something that all Plymothians should be proud of and all visitors should envy. *EH 27 Sept 2003*

HOE BANDSTAND No powerful electrical amplifiers in those days and so the crowds all sat or stood in a circle around the bandstand. In later years two styles of deckchairing appeared - with and without arm rests! The armrests cost extra and you could reserve a seat in advance for the inner rings of the circle. However strip away the stand and the period costume and there are very few discernable differences between the two views. The profile of Staddon Heights is thankfully little changed, even the old firing range wall on the horizon, which wasn't even in use in the Then picture, has survived. Meanwhile, Mount Batten has recently been reinstated to appear more like it did at the beginning of the twentieth century than at any other point since. The long redundant octagonal watch-tower is another curious survivor while the top of the Plymouth Dome represents the most obvious modern feature on the landscape. *EH 06 May 2000*

PLYMOUTH HOE Plymouth Hoe is undoubtedly one of Plymouth's finest assets and has been ever since tourism has been an important part of the local economy. In the early 1880s, once the impact of the railways made itself fully felt and the towns hotel stock had increased in both number and size, so the City Fathers looked to enhancing their most obvious attraction. Gardens were laid out, memorials erected, to Drake and the Armada, Smeaton's tower was rescued from its unsafe footings and the Belvedere was created. In the 100 years since little has changed, a large memorial was erected and extended to remember the lives of the naval personel who lost their lives in the two World Wars and, more recently, a smaller memorial was erected for the airmen. But apart from the Dome and the currently neglected Tinside, little has been spent on major projects here to attract visitors on into the twenty-first century. As can be seen by comparing these two images, little has changed in the sixty or so years that separate them, except that about half-way through that period another hotel was built to the west of the Grand. *EH 01 May 1998*

LOCKYER STREET Who remembers this splendid entrance to the Hoe Promenade at the top of Lockyer Street? Brightly illuminated with different coloured neon strips, it takes us back to a time before the war when the main route onto the Hoe was straight up from Derry's Clock. Nowadays, with so many ways of approaching this spectacular open space, it's hard to imagine what it was like before the war; before the creation of Armada Way, when Citadel Road had houses along both sides of its middle section (seen here running from the middle to the far right of the early picture) and indeed before Madeira Road was cut around the front of the Citadel and pedestrians had to negotiate the Cage Walk to make their way around from Sutton Harbour. But what was this grand gateway created for? Was it for the opening of Tinside Pool, was it for George (V) and Mary's Jubilee in 1935 or was it for George VI's Coronation in 1937? Or was it simply to attract the tourists. *EH 24 April 1999*

HOE CAFÉ It's funny how one generally assumes that once a piece of land has been developed for some commercial purpose then that's it, never again shall it be green, but curiously enough, that notion has been confounded twice in recent years on the Hoe. Remember the Hoe Theatre? For 20 years it was the principal municipal stage in Plymouth – now there's nothing to remind you it existed. And there's a similar story with the Hoe Café, that curious blot on the landscape was removed around the same time, early 1980s. Now a pleasant sensory garden sits alongside the war memorial. Elsewhere, there is grass where once a part of Citadel Road ran, and where the bandstand once was. What other changes does the future have in store for the Hoe and the Foreshore? And if there is a major development of the foreshore over the next few years, what will the history books have to say about it in 10 or 15 years time. *EH 30 Dec 2000*

HOE THEATRE Our Then picture dates from the last year that the Hoe Theatre was open and indeed standing - how long ago do you think that was? It was in 1982, the same year that the Theatre Royal opened on Royal Parade. For twenty years this unremarkable little theatre on the Hoe had been one of the main entertainment venues in town and thousands of visitors were treated here to the annual Summer show; it was originally opened as the Hoe Summer Theatre. For all its shortcomings these, at times, cold and draughty premises were a marked improvement on the marquee that had been its predecessor and many successful pantos, talent shows and winter shows, were seen here, particularly towards the end of its days when the Plymouth Theatre Company staged a number of fine productions at the venue. Today it is hard to imagine that the theatre itself was anything more than a temporary flight of fancy as that part of the Hoe looks much the same as it did before its concrete base was ever laid. *EH 30 Jan 1999*

HOE STATUES Drake's statue and that of Britannia, commemorating the great victory over the Spanish Armada, both appeared on the Hoe in the 1880s. It was the decade that saw the first formal laying out of that spectacular open space. Since then, changes have few, as you can see from these two images separated by more than 80 years. The First World War Memorial, extended after the Second World War, occupies an appropriately prominent position; otherwise the differences are down to fashion and foliage. *EH 24 Jan 2004*

CITADEL GATE Given that the Citadel Gate has been standing little changed for some 333 years it's no great surprise to find that this view has not altered substantially over the last 66 years. Our pre-war shot shows rather more men on the gate than you're likely to find today, however, today's guard is probably a lot more heavily armed! Note the buildings inside are much the same today too. *EH 03 Jan 2004*

MARINE BIOLOGICAL ASSOCIATION At first glance, you'd be hard pushed to tell that more than seventy years separates these images. The cars are perhaps the obvious give-away, but, if you look closely, the 70s style architecture of the extension to the premises of the Marine Biological Association is also quite striking. There is also an upwards addition to the main building between the two squarish end blocks. Otherwise you might be forgiven for thinking the devastation visited upon so much of the city during the war had passed this area by. In fact, the MBA sustained a fair bit of damage. Opened in June 1888, this was the first home to an aquarium in Plymouth. It was this, coupled with the reputation and enthusiasm of certain members of the association here that led to the National Marine Aquarium being built around the corner on the edge of Sutton Harbour. *EH 23 Oct 1999*

PHOENIX WHARF Over 100 years ago, in 1895, Phoenix Wharf Pier was opened as a free public landing space and since then certain aspects of this view have changed very little. Already, by that stage, two of the large Coxside gasholders had been erected, one earlier that year and the other in 1884. The squat square-shaped building to the right was a few years off becoming the home of the Mayflower Sailing Club (just after World War One) but there were still a few traces here of the site's earlier uses. Back in 1975 this had still been a part of the main victualling yard for the Navy (it was succeeded by the development at Stonehouse in the 1830s). After that it was substantially employed as the main Emigration Depot for the South West. Not all of the old victualling buildings were used in that way though, and some of them lent themselves to private food manufacture. For years, many millions of biscuits were produced here – city alderman George Frean (later of Peak Frean) started a manufactory here and was later followed by the Serpell's biscuit factory. The greatest changes, of course came in the 1980s when the old Queen Anne's Battery site was cleared and developed for yachtsmen. *EH 28 Aug 1999*

COMMERCIAL WHARF The principal features are much the same, and the similarities are fairly obvious, but there are so many changes to see. All around the water's edge, from North Quay around to Coxside, the old buildings have come down. In the case of the China House they have been extensively refurbished inside and out. Back in 1958, a clear Commercial Wharf was still a comparative novelty. Now it is hard to picture the factories and bakeries that once lined the waterfront. *EH 03 April 2004*

WATCH HOUSE Our Then view looks deceptively contemporary in picture postcard form as it has been hand-tinted. The date on the postmark however is 1909, making the view almost 100 years old. Certainly there have been dramatic changes here, clearance of the buildings to the left began in the early thirties, especially the old Watch House on the west end of West Pier. Just after that the Mayflower Memorial was erected at the top of the so-called Mayflower Steps. *EH 11 Oct 2003*

MAYFLOWER STEPS The biggest difference here seems to be that in one shot the tide is high, in the other it isn't – but look again and changes are many at the Mayflower Steps. Now you can walk through the Mayflower Steps Memorial on to a fine semi-circular viewing platform. In much the same way, you can now walk around the splendid seventeenth-century warehouse that is now the China House pub. Other significant changes include the arrival of the 'prawn' sculpture on the end of West Pier; the construction of the lock gates (just our of the picture to the right) at the entrance to Sutton Pool; and the new fish market, built on land reclaimed from the sea in front of the old coal wharves below Teats Hill. *EH 23 December 2000*

MAYFLOWER STONE

Up until 1891 there was no obvious indicator that this part of the Barbican was, give or take a few yards, the last bit of terra firma that the Pilgrim Fathers would have stood on, in September 1620, prior to their historic Atlantic crossing to new Plymouth. For over forty years this stone (since moved nearer the memorial) and the tablet in the wall adjacent, were the only reminders, then some seventy years ago the Lord Mayor, E. Stanley Leatherby unveiled the colonnaded memorial. More recently it was transformed further when an opening was made in the wall and an attractive balcony was created. *EH 28 Sept 2004*

THE LOCK GATES There was a natural rock ridge upon which East and West Piers were created back in the 1790s and a chain used to be hauled across the divide to stop unwelcome visitors entering the harbour. Since the mid-1990s that process has been more formally controlled by the operation of the impressive lock gates, gates which have rendered Sutton Harbour navigable at all states of the tide. Around the harbour's perimeter other changes are equally impressive; the Fish Market was relocated on reclaimed land here in 1995 and three years later the National Marine Aquarium became the City's latest, and most impressive, attraction. Further to that has been the development of waterside apartments and offices, where once there were warehouses and factories.

WATCH HOUSE Perhaps one day the waterside here will be lined with buildings as it was at the beginning of last century and throughout the previous one. Accommodating the port's first victualling offices originally, they were later used for more commercial operations, notably the manufacturing of biscuits. The buildings are long gone now, as is the old police Watch House on the right, which came down in the early thirties prior to the construction of the Mayflower memorial portal.

A splendid example of a Then, Then, Then and Now across this page and the next as not only the Watch House disappears, but also the Mayflower Hotel, the site of which was clear for many years after the war. Eventually the Acropolis Restaurant was built there and today it is the Mayflower Visitor Centre that occupies the very same plot.

WEST PIER While on the one hand the Barbican is undoubtedly one of the oldest and least changed parts of the modern city, there can be few places that have seen so many dramatic alterations as the site alongside the Harbourmaster's offices. Prior to the Second World War, the impressive, four-storey Mayflower Hotel (formerly known as the Brunswick) stood here. But this was one of the few Barbican locations to take a direct hit during the Blitz, and for many years after the war there was a vacant plot here. Then in the 1960s a modern, and somewhat incongruous, structure appeared and served as a restaurant for the best part of forty years. Just a few years ago it was demolished and the new Mayflower Visitor Centre was erected in its place. *EH 16 April 2002*

CAMBER'S COURT There's no date on the picture but the hairstyles and clothing suggest the late 1940s, possibly even 1950s. The old picture shows Camber's Court and on the back of it we read "most of the houses in the court are now empty, ladies come up from Cooksley Court to have a chat and, of course, have their picture taken." Both Camber's and Cookley's Courts were off Castle Street, between there and Lambhay Street. They were ancient and cramped developments and were replaced after the war with the new flats, seen here from the end of Lambhay Street in our Now picture, and, as can be seen, they still have pleasant open areas tucked away behind them. *EH 05 May 1998*

LAMBHAY STREET The plaque on the remaining fragment of stonework here suggests that this is part of the original "castle quadrant" of Plymouth. It stands at the foot of Lambhay Street and one hundred years ago served as a dwelling house for a large family, many of whom we see here. Today only a very small part remains and although it is believed to be part of the original mediaeval castle – the one that gave us the four towers of our civic crest – experts are not convinced that this is anything other than part of a later internal building and not part of a tower, or even the gatehouse. Beyond the modern flat development that now straddles the street there is one of the few other early structures in Lambhay Street – the quaint, eighteenth-century Fisherman's Arms. *EH 05 May 1998*

26

EAST PIER With the exception of the rebuilding on the site of the earlier post-war redevelopment - that was the Acropolis and is now the Mayflower Centre – there is little major change to the skyline and the buildings below. The foreground however, and East and West Pier themselves, are barely recognisable. Who would have thought, standing here just twenty years ago that this vantage point was to see greater changes in the two decades that followed than it had in the two hundred years that had elapsed since Admiral John MacBride had seen the piers take shape. *EH 18 Oct 2003*

THE BARBICAN The vantage point is unmistakable and yet the differences are quite profound when you examine these two images. Taking us back almost thirty years the Then picture shows a Barbican where the fish market dominated the western side of the harbour. The now long gone ice-house, where Dartington's pyramid-shaped glass blowing works now stands, had yet to be built and all manner of vehicles clogged the seaward side of the road. In the distance the most familiar landmarks still punctuate the skyline: the spire of Charles Church, the tower of Charles with St Matthias and that impressive educational premises that was then Sutton High School for Boys (and before that Regent Street School) and is now a part of the further education establishment in the city. In the middle distance we see yet more significant changes as large blocks of harbourside flats now dominate the front elevation of North Quay and where there was just an open expanse of harbour there is now a large and thriving marina. *EH 24 July 1999*

ACROPOLIS RESTAURANT It will make an interesting Then and Now in a year or so for the future of the restaurant opposite the Mayflower steps is not thought to be a long one now. Earmarked for some time now as the soon-to-be-built Mayflower Visitor Centre, this was one of the first examples of major investment in the Barbican after the war and was an early indication that the times down here were a-changing. Also we now see ticket dispensers, reminding us that there are now far more cars on the road and that space today is at a premium. For almost 40 years the incongruous 60s structure seen in our Then picture served as a restaurant, the Acropolis, and in our more recent Then image, we see the revamped building facing a short future. *EH 29 Jan 2000*

THE FISH MARKET This delightful Victorian scene of sail-powered fishing boats unloading at the Barbican, before the old fish market had even been built (it was completed in 1896), highlights the old horse-power situation perfectly with a dozen or so horse-drawn carts waiting to take fish to other parts, and other modes of transport – the train. In our Now picture, with its stream of highly-horse-powered cars, it is strange to reflect that the building with the pyramid roof was operational, with its glass-blowing furnaces, for an even shorter period than the 1960s ice house that stood on the same site. *EH 19 July 2003*

BARBICAN The Barbican came through the Blitz lightly compared to the City Centre, but one of the numerous sites to be hit was just to the left of our Then picture, above the first boat in sail. Today, laid out for public seating, the area is alongside the Island House, clearly visible in both shots. So too is the old fish market, which was comparatively new when the earlier picture was taken. For some years now this has been home to Dartington Glassworks, although the intriguing structure to the left of the old market has recently been vacated by the glass blowers themselves. *EH 17 Sept 2002*

FISH MARKET Photographed in the late 1950s for our Then shot, we see the old fish market before the 1960s icehouse was added and clearly some years before the old 1890s building was superceded by the current 1990s affair on the other side of Sutton Harbour. Apart from the changes effected by Dartington Glass, the other differences are a little more subtle – but after forty five years of great change on the Barbican you wouldn't expect everything to be quite the same from any angle. *EH 17 April 2004*

RAILWAY OFFICES The wording on the wall of the 'London South Western Railway Receiving Office for Goods and Parcels for all Parts', is not as clear as it once was but then that's hardly surprising considering that the building hasn't been used for that purpose for over sixty years. However what is perhaps surprising is that attempts to preserve the wording are ongoing, courtesy of the Barbican Association. The changes in fashion and street furniture are obvious enough, but apart from the buildings this side of the Island House and the glass-blowing block of Dartington Glass, the structural changes are more subtle.

CAP'N JASPERS The years roll by remarkably quickly, it doesn't seem that long ago that fish was being landed on this side of Sutton Harbour and Cap'n Jasper was serving up hot and freshly cooked Mackerolls. Today, a decade on, both are still very much in business, the fish market having moved to impressive new premises on the other side of the water and Jaspers into less temporary accommodation (the old Barbican Police Station), which is almost visible through the glass walls of the converted, late-Victorian, fish market building, which now houses Dartington Glass. Meanwhile, the parking arrangements have changed and pedestrians can now roam the vast cobbled areas of Quay Road and the Barbican with a greater sense of ease. *EH 22 Sept 2001*

ISLAND HOUSE A century or so separates the images and yet this splendid four-hundred-year-old building looks in better shape than ever. In the hands of the Bayly family since 1786, it was, as can clearly be seen, a Ship Chandler's 100 years ago and indeed fulfilled that role from around 1850 through till the 1920s. It had been many things before and has been since. For the last decade or so the ground floor has seen service as a Tourist Information Centre, but the property is best known to locals and visitors alike as one of the buildings most likely to have housed some of the Pilgrim Fathers on their brief visit here in 1620. Indeed there has been a plaque (maintained and upgraded by the Barbican Association) naming the Mayflower's passengers on the side of Island House, for many years. *EH 30 July 2002*

QUAY ROAD Time was when many of the buildings surrounding the Barbican had sea water lapping their walls. Today few do, as over the last three hundred years there has been a gradual process of quay building as water transport has given way to wheeled transport. Just over a hundred years ago our vantage point here would have been a watery one. Quay Road having been created expressly to serve the Fish Market that was built here in the 1890s and which one hundred years later, when the market moved, became the local home for Dartington Glassworks. Quay Road was pedestrianised around the same time.

NEW STREET Almost bulldozed in the nineteen-fifties, along with so many other post-war survivors of ancient Plymouth, New Street is a remarkable mix of old, new and really ancient. The two properties behind the lady in the Then picture survived until the nineteen-eighties, the building directly behind the man had gone a little earlier, but thanks to the Old Plymouth Society and its later off-shoot the Barbican Association, there are a number of fine sixteenth and seventeenth century houses here. Along with them, one or two great grey warehouses from the early nineteenth century and a number of developments from different parts of the twentieth century survive, including the most recent, John Sparke House, named after the man who first developed the street over 400 years ago. *EH 11 Jan 2003*

ELIZABETHAN HOUSE New Street was new four hundred years ago and although it was not really developed for housing until the days of the first Queen Elizabeth it is nevertheless one of the oldest thoroughfares in Plymouth. Its cobbled street surface is a grade two listed structure - not that much respect is paid to that fact when it is dug up by the various bodies responsible for gas, water, electricity or telecommunications - and many of the properties in the street are of even higher listing. Not that many of them would be there today had it not been for the efforts of the Barbican Association in the 1950s. Newly-formed then to stop the local authorities demolishing so many historic properties, the Association still own many properties in the street today and are currently in the process of restoring several of them for future generations. The roots of the Association itself were to be found in the efforts of that dedicated group who, some years earlier, had been responsible for the preservation of the Elizabethan House, next to the Green Lanterns, back in 1929. *EH 14 Aug 1999*

PIN LANE Apart from the lamppost at the top of the steps and a few changes in personnel, there appears to be little to chronicle the passage of 60 years which separate these two images. When the wartime photograph was taken, New Street, at the top of Pin Lane, was a densely populated thoroughfare. Fifteen to twenty years later and most of the properties in the street had been scheduled for demolition. Happily, however, they were saved; the older premises further down the street by the then newly-founded Barbican Association and the buildings here by Dennis and Mary Browning, who bought them in 1962. In the years that followed, 44 and 43 New Street became listed buildings and several writers, artists and craftsmen and women started businesses in the many rooms here – including me, Chris Robinson – Plymouth Prints first opening for trade here in 1978 (moving to 34 New Street in 1984). Standing on the site of a former medieval monastery, Greyfriars, the Georgian façade we see today covers two older Elizabethan cottages - which have been much altered and extended over the years. Today the West Devon Gallery trades out of 43, while the proposals for 44 look set to take it full circle and see it converted back to domestic accommodation. *EH 31 July 1999*

THE HOE GATE The only one of Plymouth's town gates to have survived into the era of the photograph was the Hoe Gate. 'New Built' by Timothy Alsop in the mid-seventeenth century it was eventually pulled down in 1863, as part of the Corporation's drive to widen local thoroughfares although 'decency' was also said 'to forbid its continued existence.' Clearly Citadel Road now sits either side of the gate site, however a good visual clue linking the two images in the wall in the foreground.

SOUTHSIDE STREET There's no date on our Then picture, but it is after the war and some years before 1968 when the present Queen's Arms was constructed on the corner of Friar's Lane. Designed by Jim Luxton, it was built to similar overall dimensions to the earlier building on this site, which had long been known as the Queen's Arms. That wasn't its original name, however, and it is quite likely that the building, which for many years has sported a sign with the arms of Queen Elizabeth I, was known several centuries ago as the Plymouth Arms. Southside Street was a busy thoroughfare in early Tudor times, and was the main route from town to the old castle. But formal development of the Barbican end of the street happened, for the most part, in late Elizabethan times. The building on the left here, on the corner of Pin Lane, is thought to have been built for one of Drake's captains who fought against the Armada. *EH 21 Feb 1999*

SOUTHSIDE STREET It is 1966 and early one morning in Southside Street on Plymouth's Barbican, the red and white Mother's Pride van is making a delivery. Slightly ahead of it, there's the milkman on his round, his electric float parked just outside the Galaxy Gallery. Galleries and craft shops were just starting to make a major impact in this area. However, apart from Jacka's Bakery further along on the right hand side, no business has survived longer in this part of the street than Yarmouth Stores. The shop's sign has been outside the premises for more than 100 years. Originally known as "South Side", (it was very much an Elizabethan suburb) the street was paved in 1584. Around 400 years later the paving was extended significantly as the street was made more pedestrian-friendly. Apart from some sign changes and a few cosmetic alterations, the street has altered little over the last century. Indeed, one or two buildings have barely altered since the street was first developed all those years ago. *EH 20 May 1999*

SOUTHSIDE STREET The cars are the biggest clue to the passage of time here, as the buildings look much the same as they did 30, 40 or even, from this angle, 100 years ago. Indeed a hundred years ago the shop with the hanging sign, Yarmouth Stores, was already trading here and had been for some time, making it one of the oldest established businesses in Plymouth today. But not quite the oldest in Southside Street. That honour goes to Jacka's Bakery, which has been trading as a bakery here for more than 400 years. Let's not forget Plymouth Gin either, another Southside Street business that was established a short distance to the west of this spot back in 1793. In those days, wheeled transport would have been an occasional rather than a regular sight and it is interesting to note that in recent years there has been an effort to make the street as pedestrian friendly as possible. *EH 07 Oct 2000*

JACKA'S BAKERY It is a sad fact of life that small independent bakeries are disappearing around the country at an alarming rate. In Plymouth, on the Barbican, Southside Street's ancient bakery is just about the only one left in the area. It is also the oldest commercial working bakery in the country and, remarkably, it has only changed hands a few times. For centuries it passed down through various members of the Fownes family, with Frank Fone Warren (FF Warren), the last of that line here, selling to John Jacka in the early twentieth century. In the 1980s John's nephew, Hugh, sold the business to the current proprietor, Roger Compton, and recently he has had the frontage restored to something like its Victorian appearance - as evidenced by our Then picture. Note that 100 years ago the bakery's neighbours were Hingston Brothers – Blockmakers – originally, however, the Elizabethan bakery stood alone and there are window frames evident on both sides of the building – as well as back and front. *EH 03 Feb 2001*

THE MARITIME The door of the Maritime has become another window, as this Southside Street hostelry has expanded, not only sideways but lengthways as well, taking in its former neighbour at the back. The move then gave the pub a second street-facing entrance, this time on the Parade. Meanwhile further down the streetscape two more pubs have appeared since our Then picture was taken, the Distillery and the Gog Magog

PIERMASTERS The Barbican has long been cherished for its quaint old buildings and narrow streets, but who, thirty years ago would have thought that active steps would have been taken to make one of its main streets even narrower still? But that is exactly what has happened here as greater emphasis has been put on pedestrian pleasure at the expense of the motorsist and parking places. None of which has done anything to deter the restauranteur and the publican from heading this way, but it has had an impact on the rest of the retail activity here.

QUAY ROAD The cars have been bannished, and, in the summer, Quay Road is transformed into a cosmopolitan mass of people socializing around the wooden tables, giving this part of the Barbican a Continental appearance. The great, wide, cobbled thoroughfare lends itself admirably to the purpose and it is worth reflecting that this part of Plymouth has a greater area of cobbled surface than any other part of Britain. For several centuries, the distinctive Three Crowns pub has looked out over the harbour here, while the Custom House alongside it has been a neighbour since 1820. The Civic Centre building, which dominates the skyline to the left, is one of the more recent additions to this view and will, in all probability, be the first to disappear in years to come.

BARBICAN Changes on the Barbican over the last few years have been drastic in some places and minimal in others. One overriding aspect, though, has been a slow move away from the point of production - there are fewer jobs in manufacturing industries, and a move towards tourism and housing. Consequently, the Barbican is a prettier, less busy place than it was thirty years ago when Tope's sailmaking premises, here, was just one of many manufacturing or employment places in the area. *EH 17 May 2003*

BARBICAN LAMPPOST The Lamp-stand is the same, but the newer lamp looks older and more in keeping with its support unit. More than thirty years separate the two images and in that time, sadly, Robert Lenkiewicz has come, and gone, from the Barbican. His marvellous mural, begun in the early 1970's had yet to be painted and now it's long past its best – but hopefully the artist's legacy will live on. The approach to the Parade has been re-cobbled and Harbour Sports has long since replaced Dunstan and Sons' bonded store and off-licence. Otherwise, its pretty much business as usual and the flats, which were new then are very much part of the scene today. *EH 26 April 2003*

HARBOUR SPORTS The Blitz and the subsequent redevelopment of the Barbican have led to a few changes in the street pattern here on the edge of the Parade, but not too many. We still get a clear view across Vauxhall Street towards Looe Street along the side of what is now Harbour Sports. There is a new opening on to the Parade though, here to our left, and the "new" flats are not so new any more. Quite what the occasion for our Then shot was is not clear, but certainly it dates from a time when motoring was one of the latest crazes and from a time when windsurfing, surfing and bodyboarding, with the attendant man-made boards and rubberised wetsuits were still very much a pastime of the future. One hundred years ago the idea of such an assembly of metal motors on the cobbles would have seemed most odd, who knows how it will all seem in another hundred years. *EH 21 July 2001*

THE PARADE The cobbled surface suggests that Parade Ope is considerably older than it is, for as our Then picture shows the northern side of the Parade itself used to run from the bottom end of High Street (out of picture to the left – and currently running right through the new flats) to Exchange Street – where the Three Crowns still stands. Indeed from Harbour Sports east, all the old buildings survive, it is only these here that we are missing today.

HIGH STREET Curiously enough the street line itself is little altered but at first glance it appears there is nothing else to connect the two - even the name is different today. But, look again and you can see quite clearly that the building at the top of this bit of High Street in the old picture, is the same building that we see directly above the Ford estate car in this Now picture of Buckwell Street. That building, known for some time as the Old Well Eating House, is like the well itself very old, as were all of the buildings depicted in the 1890s photograph. High Street, after all, is/was one of the oldest streets in Plymouth and at one time was one of the most important, hence the name generally conferred on similar streets in other towns - High Street. The buildings on the right were cleared in the 1930s to make way for the flats that are still there today. The properties on the right survived redevelopment then and many of them survived the war too, but they didn't manage to survive the post-war re-planning, and, along with many other Tudor and similar period buildings were pulled down in the 1950s. *EH 20 Feb 1999*

NOTTE STREET Apart from the layout of the streets, there are two clear common elements here. First the block between St Andrew Street and the bottom of Buckwell Street (from the Spar Shop down in our Now photo), and second, the chimney-stack of the Plymouth Gin Distillery (to the right in both pictures). Otherwise, although the building heights are similar, the structures we see in the Now picture are all post-war, as indeed they are in our Then picture. Look closely and you will see several old buildings cleared, perhaps unnecessarily, in the late 1950s. *EH 28 July 2001*

ST ANDREW STREET/NOTTE STREET The whole of the western corner of St Andrew Street and Notte Street has long since gone and has been replaced, some way behind the original building line, by a modern office block. The eastern corner, however, survives largely intact. Some of the fancy mouldings above the top windows have gone, most notably above the corner premises itself, but otherwise this section of Notte Street is, remarkably enough, much as it was in our Then picture, which dates from 1937. Sixty years on, though, little else of old Notte Street survives and the redevelopment around this particular view is very marked, such that the comparison here, perhaps, gives an artificial notion of the scale of change. It's interesting to note the buses turning into Notte Street, the old one from St Andrew Street when the street ran right up through to town and the other from the new Hoe Approach Road – a route no one could have envisaged being made before the war. *EH 16 Oct 1999*

NOTTE STREET The street line is much the same and the terraced block in the distance is little changed either, otherwise it is difficult to equate these two images of Notte Street. The former dates from 1937 and shows not only different streets and buildings but a different era for transport. This was a time when there were very few private cars on the road, the horse and cart was still a regular sight - as indeed was the man and (hand)cart. The streets intersecting Notte Street here, incidentally, are Catherine Street to the left and Zion Street to the right, with the entrance to Finewell Street just a little further down on the left. Now wider and more open, we see the present day Notte Street has new buildings set back from the original line with the Unitarian Church rather pleasantly framed by a group of trees. *EH 19 June 2000*

NOTTE STREET Although it's on the fringes of the modern city centre and seemingly outside the area we think of as being affected by the 1943 Plan for Plymouth there's little here, at first glance, overlapping the pre and post-war city centre. However, here the essential line of Notte Street has been preserved and many of the side roads feeding it are still around today – and in some instances one or two original buildings survive. In this particular vista, however, it's hard to find more than kerb stones that are common to both. *EH 26 June 2004*

POPHAMS FURNITURE STORE Pophams was undoubtedly one of Plymouth's premier stores pre-war and for a few years after it; "Where the West Buys the Best" was its boast. It was based in Bedford Street with a furniture repository here, in nearby Notte Street. Today the line of the old Notte Street remains pretty much the same but from this particular vantage point, little remains that is common to both views. *EH 03 July 2004*

NOTTE STREET NAAFI Remarkably these two images are separated by just over fifty years. Our Then picture was taken in July 1952, the year that the Services' new NAAFI club was opened by Princess Margaret, with the then Lord Mayor, Henry Wright. As you can see although this building had been completed work on Armada Way itself was still under way. The hands on the clock tower had moved around a fair few times by 1970 when the Holiday sprang up on the empty site behind it. By which time Armada Way had taken pretty much the shape we know now – except that the Ark Royal anchor, just out of view to the right here, had yet to appear – it was presented to the City in April 1980. Curiously enough within a few months of this Naval memento appearing outside the NAAFI the usage of the building changed, as, in July 1980, this officially became the Plymouth School of Architecture, now very much a part of the University of Plymouth.

ST ANDREW STREET It is a street of two halves today and has been since it was dissected in the late 1970s by the construction of the city magistrates' court. St Andrew Street is one of the oldest thoroughfares in Plymouth. When so much of the city's early street pattern was altered in the immediate post-war planning, it is a shame that this historic cobbled stretch running down from the back of the ancient parish church should have been broken up in this way. But the court building is one of the more inspired pieces of post-war architecture in the city centre, and the space around it is gradually coming into its own, with planting and pedestrian-friendly areas. The southern section we see here relies primarily on the underrated seventeenth century Merchant's House museum, and the pub opposite, for its character. *EH 30 Sept 2000*

ST ANDREW STREET Leading down from the back of Plymouth's parish church, St Andrew Street is one of the oldest thoroughfares in the city today, although since the late 1970s it has been a street of two halves, thanks to the creation of the Magistrates Court. Before that, and before the war, as we can see in our Then picture from 1937, the street ran straight up to Bedford Street, just a little to the west of its junction with Old Town Street. In this particular section we see three surviving buildings the seventeenth century Merchant's House, the Swan (Pen and Parchment) Hotel and the erstwhile Co-operative on the corner, now a Spar shop. *EH 01 Oct 2002*

THE MERCHANT'S HOUSE Almost bizarrely the newer picture shows us more clearly how the building used to be, for over the years 33 St Andrew Street has been much altered and adapted to suit its various occupants. Built as a wealthy merchant's house at the turn of the sixteenth and seventeenth century – although it is thought there was a house on the site in the early 1500s – the man most likely to be that wealthy merchant was William Parker. Parker was Mayor of Plymouth in 1601-2 and at least another two Plymouth mayors lived here in the seventeenth century. A taxi office, a shop, and a shoe repairer's, were the lot of the building in more recent years, until 1972, when the City Council began a five-year restoration of the premises, bringing it back into line with its original appearance. Open to the public today the house is full of fascinating insights into Plymouth's past. *EH 05 May 1998*

ST ANDREW STREET Leading down from the back of Plymouth's parish church, St Andrew Street is one of the oldest thoroughfares in the city today, although since the late 1970s it has been a street of two halves, thanks to the creation of the Magistrates Court. Before that, and before the war, as we can see in our Then picture from 1937, the street ran straight up to Bedford Street, just a little to the west of its junction with Old Town Street. In this particular section we see three surviving buildings the Merchant's House, the Swan (Pen and Parchment - now Big Wigs) Hotel and the erstwhile Co-operative on the corner, now a Spar shop. *EH 01 Oct 2002*

THE TURK'S HEAD Thought to be the oldest inn site in Plymouth, here from the Middle Ages through to 1860, stood the delightful old Turk's Head. Many thought at the time that it should not be pulled down – it was, after all, believed to be the oldest public house in Plymouth. But sadly it was and the following year the Abbey Hotel rose up on the site. Renamed in the last few years "Kitty O'Hanlon's," the St Andrew Street hostelry has had many changes of neighbours over the years but the granite sets in the street itself still help convey a feeling of those former times. *EH 05 May 1998*

MUMFORD'S In 1933 Mumford's new car showrooms were constructed on the site of a delightful block of Tudor properties known collectively as Abbey Place. St Andrew Street in those days ran straight down from the eastern end of St Andrew's Church down to Notte Street. Forty-six years later, however, Mumford's itself had disappeared and in its place the new Plymouth Magistrates Court had appeared. An altogether much larger development this new 1979 structure, opened by Prince Charles, effectively cut St Andrew Street in two as the middle section was completely cleared. The bottom half of the street now starts with the Merchant's House on one side and the Pen and Parchment, formerly the Swan Hotel, on the other. At the top the most notable recent change has been the conversion of the old insurance buildings into the Café Rouge. *EH 28 Nov 1998*

CAFÉ ROUGE The vantage point isn't quite the same but the features are unmistakable. The dark silhouette of St Andrews Church dominates the right-hand side of both images and although there is still a substantial amount of open land to the north of the building, the layout has changed. Note, however, the two gate-posts, both exactly as they were pre-war. Back then Old Town Street extended further south and on the left you can see where it reached down to Whimple Street. The north side of Whimple Street, like old Old Town Street, has been removed, thanks to the Blitz and the subsequent redevelopment, the south side remains largely as it was, although there have been many changes of use. Among them the transformation of the Insurance buildings into the Café Rouge.

SPOONER'S CORNER It's difficult with no common reference point between these two images to be sure you've got exactly the right spot and even more difficult to persuade anyone today that this is what you would have seen from this vantage point just over sixty years ago. In our then picture (1937) we're looking across the bottom of Old Town Street with the north side of the western end of Whimple Street to our right. Today, the modern Old Town Street does not stretch that far south and only a part of the south side of Whimple Street remains. *EH 18 Mar 2000*

WHIMPLE STREET Although they stand on the same site, in the same line and proportion, the buildings to the right in these views are not the same, the modern replacements however do represent one of the more sensitive post-war developments on the fringe of the modern city centre. The great pity though is that beyond this point the medieval line of Whimple Street has been totally lost, thanks to the construction of an electricity sub-station and the Job Centre on this site. The pre-war building that formerly occupied this position was the mid-Georgian Guildhall (always considered to be inadequate for its purpose). This structure, in turn, stood on the site of Plymouth's earlier, Jacobean Guildhall and before that this was the site of the town's Market Cross, at the junction of Whimple Street, Looe Street and High Street, all in all a very significant site in the history of Plymouth and one that is quite lost to us today.

LOOE STREET Plymouth lost more Elizabethan and Jacobean buildings after the Second World War than it did during that horrific time of aerial devastation … and it would have lost even more had it not been for the work of a dedicated band of local solicitors, accountants, estate agents and businessmen who created an organisation known as the Barbican Association. This group saved many key Barbican buildings from almost certain demolition, including properties in the Parade, New Street and here in Looe Street. From the Arts Centre down, the southern side of Looe Street contains some of the city's most impressive early buildings and as a group they give us an indication of how this part of Plymouth looked centuries ago – when this area was at the very heart of the town, with the town hall, market and principal inn all at the top of the street. *EH 15 Sept 2001*

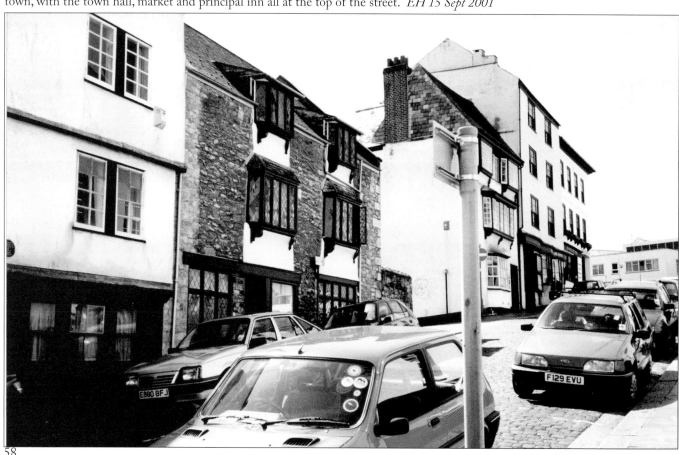

TIN LANE An interesting Then and Now set of four pictures here; the principal building featured was, for some eighty years, the Corporation Mortuary and, for most of that time, the Coroner's Court. If you look closely enough you can still see the lettering "De Morturis Nil Nisi Bonum" – "Say Nothing But Good Of The Dead", running across the frontage of the main windows Built, it seems, 100 years ago in 1898, the premises were not part of the transfer of property to the Devon authorities when local government was reorganised in the early 1970s. County policy was to hire halls for inquests where necessary and so it was decided not to buy this block, thus, in 1981, it was bought from the City Council by Eddie Barron and for a number of years his EFB Army and Navy surplus stores business operated from here. More recently, a further change has seen it become the Barbican Pine Shop. Note the refashioned windows and the alterations to the rear of the building. Tin Lane runs between the old mortuary and the Cooperage – just off Vauxhall Street. *EH 05 May 1998*

KING'S HEAD The best part of forty years separates these two images. When our Then picture was taken, Bretonside bus station and the adjacent Turnbull's garage were both fairly new. Today the Staples building is similarly new (with the ground floor restaurant having been open for over a year). However, in terms of the King's Head's history, both scenes are 'modern'. This pub has stood here for the best part of 400 years and is probably the oldest in the heart of Plymouth. *EH 20 Sept 2003*

PLAZA It is one of life's little quirks that this building opened just before the last war as the Plaza Cinema, the name coming from a Spanish word meaning a public place or square where people meet for entertainment. Quirky because in its later years as a cinema it was well-known as a place where foreign language films constituted a large part of its bill of fare. By that stage though the premises had been renamed the Studio Seven. That closed in the 1980s however, and after a spell as an indoor market with neighbouring snooker facilities the front part of this still visually-impressive building has for many years now been a popular Indian restaurant, as exotic films ultimately have given way to exotic food. *EH 10 Dec 2002*

HAWKERS If it wasn't for the vehicles and the signage, you could be forgiven for confusing which was the Then, and which was the Now. The original premises of James Hawker and Co. Ltd., were rebuilt before the Second World War and many of the architectural details echoed an earlier age than that of the earlier building. Currently occupied, on the ground floor at least, by Blackfriars Copy, David King, the proprietor, says that the only element of the site that is historically listed is the wall that we see to the left of the building in both pictures! *EH 05 April 2003*

NORTH QUAY In 1972 seventy yacht moorings were laid down off a single pontoon alongside Sutton Wharf. Within two weeks they had all been snapped up. A year later, the number of moorings was more than doubled and still the demand exceeded supply. In 1974 the number was increased to two hundred and a year later there were as many again still on the waiting list. More were added later but twenty years later there was a slight reduction in the number available, in order to accommodate the larger yachts. Currently there are 275 available moorings. *EH 05 May 1998*

SUTTON HARBOUR On the skyline the distinctive features of Sutton High School can be seen looking back across Sutton Harbour. However the school is no longer a school and the character of the Harbour it looks out on has changed enormously too. Most of the warehousing has gone or been converted and bold new housing developments dominate the waterfront. From this perspective though perhaps the biggest change is the entrance to the harbour, now controlled by lock gates.

NORTH QUAY North Quay sported the post-war Co-op warehouse and a number of other, more hastily-erected, warehouses - the China House was still a warehouse too. The lock gates were more than a decade away, as was the Aquarium and all the other recent Coxside developments. Note the fixed point landmarks on the skyline, Charles Church on the left and Charles with St Matthias to the right of what was Sutton High School. *EH 21 Feb 2004*

THISTLE PARK Fifty years ago we were about as likely to be in the way of a train (Dartmoor-Coxside line) as a car, standing here across from the Thistle Park Tavern, just over 150 years ago and this pub was a brand new development on the edge of a field of thistles. Today there is another new development on that former thistle park, the Warner Village, the pub meanwhile retains its dignified stance on this increasingly busy corner, and while only twenty years or so separates these two images there are plenty of changes. *EH 04 Oct 2003*

PLYMOUTH, THE BARBICAN.

SUTTON HARBOUR On the skyline the distinctive features of Sutton High School can be seen looking back across Sutton Harbour. However the school is no longer a school and the character of the Harbour it looks out on has changed enormously too. Most of the warehousing has gone or been converted and bold new housing developments dominate the waterfront. From this perspective though perhaps the biggest change is the entrance to the harbour, now controlled by lock gates. *EH 05 Oct 2004*

CATTEDOWN *(right)* Our then picture here is an unusual early view of from Mount Batten taken in 1887 just as Cattedown Wharf was nearing completion. Victoria and Esso Wharves were still some years away into the future and the coastline here was still largely as it had been hundreds, thousands, of years ago. At the back of it though it is interesting to see that there was more commercial and industrial development there than there is today. Long gone are the smoke-belching chimneys, Cattedown Road survives however, behind that long limestone wall - a fascinating path from the past. Over on the Mount Batten side there have been great changes too although, despite the differences in design you wouldn't readily think that the boats in our then picture are well over 100 years old. *EH 26 May 2001*

CHARLES CHURCH Isn't life strange sometimes? Take a look at these two pictures and what do you see? Charles Church, Then and Now; Then surrounded by a graveyard in the middle of a built-up part of Plymouth, with Green Street running behind us, Vennel Street off to the left and Norley Street curving around the western and northern side of the church. Now almost all of its old neighbours have gone, either blitzed, like the church, or cleared in the post-war replanning of the city centre. Inaccessible now to all but the most adventurous of pedestrians, the seventeenth-century church is preserved as a memorial to those civilians who lost their lives in the last war. Behind it we can see the skeletal 1970s car park. Unlike the stone-built church it is a concrete cancer victim - despite its comparative youth. Meanwhile the building to our left, preventing the possibility of capturing the same vantage point, is the currently vacant former Turnbull's garage. Much publicised as the first purpose-built, self-service garage in the country, it looks like surviving but a small fraction of the time that the walls of Charles Church have been dominating this view. *EH 30 Oct 1999*

CHARLES CHURCH INTERIOR Sanctioned by Charles I in 1640, work had only just begun on Charles Church when the Civil War started two years later. Nevertheless, the first wedding and the first of many thousands of baptisms were recorded here before the war and the work were over. Besieging Royalist forces at one point came within firing range of the building. But 300 years later, as thoughts were turning towards its tercentenary celebrations, Charles Church was destroyed by the first hostile action to affect the city directly since the Civil War – The Blitz. Today, the walls and tower are a memorial to the civilians killed in World War Two. Sadly, isolated on its roundabout, it is a memorial few have the chance to experience from the inside. *EH 26 Aug 2000*

TURNBULLS *(right)* Our Then picture was taken less than six years ago, but already it seems like much longer. Today, one of the most controversial developments of post-war Plymouth sits on a large part of the area featured here – The Staples/Gala Bingo building. The last remaining feature of Britain's first self-service garage, the distinctive circular showroom is, once again, operating as a showroom, this time for motorcycles. *EH 17 Jan 2004*

CHARLES CROSS ROUNDABOUT

Exactly forty years separate these two images – the earlier of which affords us one of the last glimpses of that part of Ebrington Street now occupied by the Charles Cross Police Station. Further up what is now Charles Street we can also see an unusual angle of the erstwhile Harvest Home, a little isolated, on the skyline. No traffic lights onto the roundabout in those days, but plenty if road works as the first post-war phase of redevelopment was starting to take shape here. *EH 21June03*

CHARLES STREET *(right)* Our Then picture of Charles Street dates from 1964 and the only conspicuous common element, in building terms is the one most likely still to be standing in another forty years, by which time it will have been standing for almost four hundred years – Charles Church, or at least the walls and towers of the structure. Architects plans give us some idea of what this may look like in a few years time, but nothing is certain, although of all the city centre views this is undoubtedly a prime candidate for another Then and Now feature in the not too distant future. *EH 25Oct 2003*

CHARLES CHURCH Late 1957, early 1958, that would appear to be the date of Doug Flood's study of Charles Church and the surrounding roundabout under construction. The seventeenth-century church tower isn't the only structure clad in scaffolding, however as in the middle distance we can see the National Westminster Bank approaching completion – it opened in 1958. Beyond that we can see, too, that the roof of St Andrew's Church has recently been reinstated. Coming forward in time, we can see how magnificently the tree, not even planted then, has matured and how the tree on the other side of the church has gone. The corner of the Staples building is a recent intruder on the scene. *EH 29 Oct 2002*

68

TREVILLE STREET The vantage points and the angles aren't perfectly matched, but they're not far off as we look here down Treville Street, across the junction with Kinterbury Street, in our then picture and down across the top of Breton Side in our now view. To properly match the photographers original location we'd really need to be standing in the Post Office at the counter, but outdoors seemed a better option. *EH 14 Feb 2004*

ST ANDREW'S CROSS The big crane in the distance – top right of the old photo – was probably working on the then new Drake Circus shopping complex, but we can't see it. What we can see has changed little over the last 25 years or so – except that the Post Office only occupies half of that curved building and there is now a fountain sporadically operating in the middle of St Andrew's Cross Roundabout. Oh yes, and if you look carefully through the trees in the older picture you can see cars parked along both sides of Old Town Street. *EH 05 May 1998*

ROYAL PARADE The trees were not in full leaf in our Then picture, but even if they had been, they wouldn't dominate this view to anything like the extent that they do now. Note also how the lamp-posts all appear to have grown too. As for the Royal Parade buildings, the apparent similarities belie many internal changes over the last thirty years as familiar names like Yeos, Spooners and Pophams have given way to Debenhams, Yates's, TK Maxx and the Hogshead. In the distance, further changes are evident as the Theatre Royal in our Now picture blocks out our view of the old Union Street railway bridge visible in the Then picture. That older picture, incidentally, was taken by Roy Westlake, and to find the precise point he took it from it was necessary to get out on the balcony of the National Westminster Bank building at the top of Royal Parade. *EH 16 Dec 2000*

NAT WEST BUILDING If the trees were in leaf, it would be even more difficult to compare these two images. But the distinctive bank building standing proud at the end of Royal Parade provides us with an unmistakable key to tie the two together. When our Then picture was taken, St Andrew's Church – our vantage point – had just been restored, the National Westminster Band had just been built and the remains of Charles Church (now almost lost in the trees) had just avoided demolition. And there were far fewer cars on the road, and in the car parks. *EH 10 April 2004*

SPOONER'S BUILDING As another part of post-war Plymouth falls under the hammer of the demolition men in Old Town Street, it is timely to reflect on a part of Royal Parade that will hopefully be spared the rod of redevelopment for many years. Known as Spooners until 1977, when, along with the John Yeo building, it was rebranded Debenhams (although Debenhams had owned the Spooner concern since 1929) this is a particularly fine piece of 1950s architecture. Like the rest of its Royal Parade neighbours, it bears up well when looked at in isolation. *EH 27 Mar 2004*

DINGLES It's an unmistakable corner and in all honesty it's hard to believe that fifty years separates these two images, but it does. Go back a further fifty years and the task would have been an impossible one for you'd have been standing inside a block of buildings that faced out towards the old George Street, Bedford Street and Westwell Street. In our earlier picture Dingles had only just been built and there was no signage on this elevation, nor was there an interestingly decorated and finished piece of old drain masquerading as a mosque-like advertising feature. Apart from that, however, the fashions are a bit of a give away – one wonders what they'll be like in another fifty years. *EH 20 Nov 2001*

BASKET STREET If you want to gauge how much Plymouth has changed over the last 150 years, take a look at these two contrasting views. Our Then picture on the left shows Basket Street in the middle of the last century – a thoroughfare known locally as Love Lane because it was used by courting couples on their way from the town for a walk on the Hoe. In those days, the Basket Street area was occupied by a basket factory, the workhouse, a quadrangle, a kitchen garden, a fowl run, and a large hall. It was cleared shortly after our picture was taken to make way for the new Guildhall and Municiple Building complex in 1869. Our modern picture shows the site today – Royal Parade opposite Debenhams. *EH 12 Dec 1998*

GUILDHALL SQUARE Possibly one of the most confusing parts of pre-war Plymouth for the post-war generation to make sense of is the Guildhall Square. The confusion is doubtless not helped by the fact that the old Guildhall and the Municipal Buildings shared so many architectural features and further that the Guildhall today is not quite the same as it was before the war. As can be seen from the two views here, the top of the small tower on the north-western corner of the Guildhall is much lower than it used to be and there is now a flat roof and no gable end to that part of the building immediately this side of the tower. As for the Municipal Buildings to the right, no trace survives at all; its front line is marked out approximately by the row of cars on the Royal Parade side of the car park here, the line of the lamp-posts in the foreground marking the line of the south-western tower of the Municipal Buildings in the old picture. The one other prominent feature now lost to us, of course, is the old General Post Office. An imposing late-Victorian structure, although it looks as if it neatly formed the western end of the Guildhall Square it did, in fact, stand on the other side of one of the City's busiest pre-war thoroughfares – Westwell Street. *EH 10 April 1999*

ST ANDREW'S HALL At the Western end of the Guildhall Square was, from the end of last century, the main Post Office. St Andrew's Hall, behind the tree, was just beside it and you can just see one of the entrances to the Municipal Buildings on the far right of the picture. Quite what the reason was for such a large gathering of horses and carriages we do not know, but we can be sure that those wealthy enough to own one would have been very proud of their 'state of the art' mode of transport. What, then, would they have made of the vehicles that appear in this view today and what will anyone who finds this contemporary picture in a hundred years time make of it then? The buildings facing us, incidentally, were all situated in Westwell Street which ran right to left across this view, right up to Princess Square, on a slightly different line to that of Armada Way today. *EH 05May98*

CATHERINE STREET The outline edge of the tower of St Andrew's – on the right of both pictures – links these two photographs of the top end of Catherine Street. The old workhouse and the Orphan's Aid building stood side by side for over two hundred years before the whole complex to the left was cleared to make way for the new Guildhall – a project which was completed in 1873. Since then the longest-serving residents in this part of the street have been the police. For over 60 years, between 1873 and 1935, this was Plymouth Police Headquarters, indeed the old blue lamp still hangs over the door. Time has moved on, though, and so have the police and the buildings – still owned by the Corporation – which have since been let for a variety of uses. *EH 05 May 1998*

CATHERINE STREET A product of the early Elizabethan school that thought it was a good idea to find or create work for the poor if they were unable to find it for themselves, the old Workhouse – otherwise known as the Hospital of the Poors Portion – was completed in 1630. Closely linked with St Andrew's, it stood at the top of Catherine Street opposite the graveyard and tower of the church. Above the entrance was carved the motto 'By God's helpe throughe Christ". This lintel and doorway now stands in the Elizabethan garden in New Street, as the workhouse was demolished in the late 1860s to make way for the new Guildhall. St Andrew's no longer has the same extensive graveyard around it but a number of the paving stones in our Now picture are old headstones from the old burial ground. *EH 05 May 1998*

GUILDHALL SQUARE Guildhall Square looking east – and whoever would have thought standing here in 1932 that in less than ten years the magnificent municipal building on the left would have been totally gutted by war? Or that within another twenty years all trace of it would have disappeared and it would have been replaced by a simple rectangular and relatively uninspiring structure a hundred yards away? And that next to it would be a council building higher than the city had ever seen before? Let us spare a thought, too, for St Andrew's Church and the Guildhall, both of which, in this picture, appear to have survived the horrors of war. As most Plymothians will know, both of these buildings were gutted during the Blitz and both were lucky to be reprieved and rebuilt in the late 1950s. St Andrew's was restored pretty much as it was, but the Guildhall, saw many changes, only a few of which are visible here. *EH 17April99*

ROYALPARADE There's simply nothing to compare, for nothing from this post-Blitz scene survives today, save perhaps for the merest hint of the Guildhall partly hidden behind the shell of the Municipal Buildings. In our Then picture we're looking from the bottom of the old Old Town Street with Bedford Street going off to our right and Basket Street running down the side of the Municipal Building. The distinctive Prudential Building stood longest but even it eventually fell prey to the redevelopment that has, in terms of Royal Parade, given Plymouth its unique character, for some fifty years now. *EH 18 June 2002*

ROYAL PARADE This Dougie Flood View takes us right back to 1951. Dingles is just about free of scaffolding – it opened in September that year – and to the far right of the scene we can see the backs of the remaining properties in Westwell Street. Royal Parade is laid out, but apart from Dingles there is little else fronting it, while Armada Way is in its infancy and still referred to in sections, the northern section being known as Phoenix Way. The flagpole, from which distances to and from Plymouth are measured, is there, but the water features, the Civic Centre and the subway are still a long way off. *EH 19 Nov 2002*

ARMADA WAY Almost forty years separates the two images. In our Then picture (taken by Roy Todd) Barclays Bank was pretty new, as indeed was the NAAFI building in Notte Street. The Holiday Inn (Moat House) had yet to be built and Smeaton's tower was temporarily relieved of its stripes. In the middle distance, a section of the war-damaged stretch of Windsor Terrace (between Lockyer Street and Windsor Lane) had yet to be cleared and there was a temporary car park on a part of the site of the old Princess Square. The site is now dominated by the anchor from the aircraft carrier Ark Royal. Launched in 1940, the ship's anchor was presented to the City here in 1980 by the Admiral of the Fleet, Lord Hill-Norton. Between the anchor and the cameraman's vantage-point, under the old trees of Westwell Gardens, is the ornamental fountain that nominally at least commemorates Plymouth's twinning with its delightful Spanish sister resort San Sebastian. Occupying the middle of what was Princess Square, this space, between Notte Street and Princess Street, is now known as San Sebastian Square. *EH 09 Oct 1999*

BARCLAYS BANK With its impressive sculptures and high arched windows, the Barclays Bank building off Princess Square is one of the more distinctive post-war structures in Plymouth City Centre. Our Then picture captures it in its earliest days back at the dawn of the 1950s with the newly built NAAFI building (opened by Princess Margaret in 1952) behind it. The Bank Chambers themselves were eventually completed in January 1957 when the second storey and extensive development to the east had been added. Since then there have been yet further changes to this view, most notably with the construction of the Moat House (originally the Holiday Inn), which now towers up behind the NAAFI, and the picturesque little development, with fountains, of San Sebastian Square in the pedestrianised Armada Way to the right of the car in the Then picture. *EH 04 Dec 2001*

PRINCESS STREET Sure, the topography suggests a similar angle but is there really anything here to link these two images? Well yes, there is, see the building to the left of the vehicle in the distance in the Then picture, well it's there in the same place to the left of the car park in our Now shot, and it is at the bottom of that particular stretch of Lockyer Street, and if you look carefully you can also make out, just to its left, the building directly opposite it, on this side of Lockyer Street. Meanwhile, the line formed by the row of nissen huts, on what used to be the centre of Princess Square, is the same as that formed by the dark shadow of the little fountain and pool that is now known as San Sebastian Square. The present building on the far right of the Now picture is part of the Council House. *EH 05 Mar 2002*

ARMADA WAY The post war Armada Way is taking shape, the NAAFI is complete and so too is phase one of what was Barclays Bank, but the pre-war Westwell Street is also clearly still thriving off Princess Square giving us an early fifties date of around 1952 for this picture. Note, incidentally, the unroofed Guildhall poking up above the newly-opened bank. Trees today obscure much of this vista but with fifty years separating the two images it is not really surprising. *EH 17 Dec 2002*

PRINCESS SQUARE At first glance there appear to be few visual links between the two images. But look above eyelevel and you can see the common elements quite clearly. From St Andrew's Church tower on the far right, across the Guildhall roof (note the changes, particularly in the middle), to the Guildhall tower itself and finally to the trees peeking above the buildings in Princess Square, then part of the cemetery of Westwell Gardens and now part of the landscaping outside the Civic Centre. Our earlier picture dates from 1937 and the building under construction, Humm's Garage, was sadly to be very short lived as the Blitz accounted for so much of Princess Square four years after this picture was taken. *EH 04 Dec 1999*

CATHERINE STREET It's difficult today to get exactly the same vantage point as this is an area where there has been a significant amount of redevelopment since the war. However, the juxtapositioning of the eighteenth-century Public Dispensary Building in Catherine Street, and the Guildhall tower behind it, tell us that we are at least close to where our cameraman stood in 1957 when both the Chimes Public House and the old St Andrew's School were still standing. In the event both these Blitz survivors were pulled down fairly soon after this, the pub not being replaced while the school was relocated in new premises behind the Duke of Cornwall Hotel. *EH 29 Sept 2001*

CIVIC CENTRE Undoubtedly, the foreground and probably the cars represent the biggest changes here, as this part of Armada Way has long since been further redeveloped as the fountains of San Sebastian Square now bear witness. It was all so very new forty years ago though, the scaffolding yet to come down from the soon-to-be-opened Civic Centre – HRH Queen Elizabeth II would perform the honours. The glimpse-through hoardings were still in place too and car number plates had yet to extend beyond the basic three letters and three numbers. If you look carefully enough at Roy Westlake's delightful Then picture you can just make out a motorbike with side-car too. *EH 12 May 2002*

ARMADA WAY UNDERPASS It doesn't seem like over thirty years ago that work started on the Armada Way underpass … but it is. And if anyone was lucky enough to win £430,000 on the football pools they would have been better off than many millionaires are today. Pearl Assurance House was still Pearl Assurance in those days and the National Westminster Bank was where MVC are now based, and the City Centre was more than a decade away from pedestrianisation! *EH 02 Aug 2003*

ARMADA WAY SUBWAY If you hadn't seen our Now picture, you could be forgiven for thinking that our Then picture wasn't that old – and in some respects it isn't THAT old. But it was in December 1973 that the subway under Royal Parade was opened and it rather looks as though our Then picture was taken pretty soon afterwards. In the meantime the vegetation has had time to grow and the subway has had a massive post-pedestrianisation makeover. The tiling through the subway and at the northern entrance is quite stunning, as indeed is the tiling at this end before it fell foul of the vandals. In its prime it was one of the more successful pieces of local public art and, indeed, still has much to commend it. *EH 18 Aug 2001*

ARMADA WAY 2003 marks the thirtieth anniversary of the opening of the Armada Way subway and therefore it is no great surprise to find that the planting has matured somewhat in that time. There have been changes to that planting in the meantime, however, and changes to the tiling on the surface of the underpass too. These changes have softened the landscape in many ways and it's hard now to picture this scene without them, harder still to recall this area without the subway ... and without the newspaper vendors and the strategically placed buskers. As for the more subtle changes it's interesting to note the change in the style of livery of the city's busses. *EH 12 Nov 2002*

ARMADA WAY SHRUBS First there was no loop, then vehicular access to Royal Parade from this stretch of Armada Way was denied, then the subway was constructed and the pedestrianisation came along and the cars disappeared altogether. Then the planting grew and grew and so the view from this particular vantage point became obscured. Who knows what subtle or even not so subtle changes may take place here over the next 50 years. *EH 10 May 2003*

DINGLES CORNER There's no date on our Then picture but the fact that Dingles is finished, the Guildhall is yet to be restored and a chunk of Westwell Street is still standing puts it somewhere between 1951 and 1954. Today foliage foils any attempt to precisely duplicate the vantage point, but the similarities and the changes are obvious enough. Traffic has long since ceased to run along the western side of Dingles Department store and pedestrians long since ceased to cross Royal Parade here at ground level. *EH 27 Dec 2003*

ARMADA WAY With so much of the modern city centre in place it's hard to believe that our Then picture takes us back more than forty-five years. Our photographer, Roy Westlake, can't be too precise about the date but, with the YMCA not yet built or begun at the top of Armada Way, this must be 1957 or earlier, but probably not much. Dingles has been up a few years but British Home Stores, just beyond the underground toilet block which we see under construction (Coles are the contractors), only opened in 1955. As for changes, not too many prior to pedestrianisation but see how the trees have grown and Dingles too, the extra floor being added after the 1988 fire. *EH 26 Nov 2002*

ROYAL PARADE If only walls could talk then the tower of St Andrews would doubtless be able to paint a picture of Plymouth with first hand accounts of Sir Francis Drake, the Civil War and the Second World War. From the top of the tower one would have seen it all – and perchance have survived it too. And today the mother church is still a prominent and successful feature of the modern city centre, specifically Royal Parade, with some of the best of the post-war architecture grouped along the length of its northern line facing it. *EH 26 July 2003*

ROYAL PARADE The Civic Centre was on its way up, but had only got about half way, so we're probably looking somewhere around 1961 for our "then" image. No middle fence, not so much traffic generally and more double-deckers – how times have changed in just four decades. *EH 14 July 2004*

THEATRE ROYAL Our Then picture shows a familiar view for anyone who grew up in the post-war years. We look up Lockyer Street from the bottom of Royal Parade, with the Civic Centre (out of picture to the left) just completed, but the Theatre Royal is still almost 20 years away. To the right here, in September 1963, we see the Blitz-surviving buildings from Bank of England Place, which like 190 and 191 Union Street, isolated in the middle of Derry's Cross roundabout, stood for many years after the war. *EH 12 May 2004*

GEORGE STREET Some of the changes here are more subtle than others. More than twenty years separate these two images, the first having been taken by Gerald Thomas just prior to the completion of the Theatre Royal. At that time the Lockyer Hotel still abutted the Bank, which was not then operating as a pub. More recently of course a new Travel Lodge Hotel has been built on the site of the erstwhile garage and car park opposite the ABC, which in turn stands on the site of the original Theatre Royal. *EH 12 June 2004*

DERRY'S CLOCK The common elements make for an instant comparison and thank goodness that no-one has ever succeeded in their bid to move this clock. For over 140 years now this Victorian wedding gift from William Derry has been a focal point for Plymothians, admittedly the area around it is not as busy as it once was but that is no reason to relocate. The Bank, too, has seen many changes and while I have no crystal ball I would guess that the car park behind us here has a shorter life-expectancy, even now, than these two rare nineteenth century city centre relics. *EH 10 Jan 2004*

DERRY'S CLOCK Then the Theatre Royal was on the right – now it's on the left. Our Then picture is of about 100 years ago. Foulston's Theatre fronted on to George Street, one of the principle thoroughfares of 19th century Plymouth. Now known as Old George Street (as opposed to the post-war New George Street), it only runs from here to the Bank pub, then a bank in the usual sense of the work. Behind it, the former Lockyer Tavern has long gone. Since the 1860s, Derry's clock has stood here, silent witness to many changes. Before the war, George Street ran off into town behind Derry's Clock. Now there is just a car park and the paved area around the back of the new Theatre Royal. The modern theatre was built in 1982, 45 years after its predecessor was pulled down. The car park servicing the new building now occupies the site of the old theatre. Meanwhile, the towering Civic Centre fills much of the modern skyline. *EH 13 November 1999*

THE ROYAL In the second decade of the nineteenth century many were they who thought that the decision to site Plymouth's first major theatre here was madness. There was genuine concern that no-one would want to walk that far from town - town then being centred very much around St Andrew's and Old Town Street. For a variety of reasons the theatre struggled in its early years and indeed in its later years. It was eventually pulled down in 1937 - there were not enough people supporting the establishment. The Royal Cinema was erected in its place and stands little changed, except in name and inside, today. Within four years, however, many of the buildings that had sprung up in the new heart of the town, in the years since the opening of the original theatre, had been flattened in the Blitz. Of those that survived that ordeal only a handful came through the post-war replanning, indeed, of those captured in our post-war, Then picture, only Derry's Clock Tower and the old Bank Building survive on this side of the Civic Centre - the Lockyer Tavern being the last of the older structures to go - it was pulled down in 1982. *EH 03 July 1999*

THE ABC CINEMA It opened as the Royal in 1938 on the site of the original Theatre Royal which was pulled down the previous year. As a single screen cinema and a live venue it could seat more than any Plymouth auditorium from 1963 until its conversion to a multi-screen complex in 1977. The Beatles played here twice, in 1963 and 64, around the time of our Then photo.

ATHENAEUM PLACE Andrew's Garage was a familiar landmark in Athenaeum Place both before and, for some years, after the war and while little of our Then picture survives today there are plenty of topographical clues to be had, not just from the lie of the land, but also from the cobbled road surface itself. Located just to the rear of the erstwhile Royal Cinema (built on the site of the old Theatre Royal just before the war - now better known as the ABC and visible here on the right), Athenaeum Lane still leads down around to the Athenaeum itself, although the building of that name also post-dates our 1937 Then picture as the original was destroyed in the Blitz and its replacement appeared twenty years later. *EH 28 May 2002*

ATHENAEUM RUIN The present Athenaeum building was opened on June 1, 1961 and the new entrance stands some yards back from that of the original building, at an angle of roughly 45 degrees to it. A fine example of Foulston's obsession with early Grecian architecture, the old Athenaeum had a particularly impressive front entrance, its entrance only a short distance away from his first local venture, the Theatre Royal, which was completed just six years earlier in 1813. This more unusual post-Blitz (May 1941) view of the side entrance was taken in Athenaeum Lane and the photographer would have had the old lodge of the Crescent and Crescent Gardens behind him. Now it is the premises of Foot and Bowden, solicitors, in the old Westward Television Studios. *EH 05 May 1998*

DERRY'S CROSS The Now view would have been quite different last year – before work began on the demolition of the car park off Derry's Cross and the construction of the new Travel Lodge. But then nothing lasts forever, as our Then view also demonstrates. These George Street premises were the 19th century survivors of the heavily-bombed area and came down in the late 1950s. Clearly visible in both pictures is the early 1950s Co-operative building. Relatively recently re-branded Derry's, the impressive façade has changed little. *EH 22 May 2004*

DERRYS FOUR-FACED DECEIVER

Hard to believe it's the same angle on Derry's Clock – but it is. Our own old 'four-faced-deceiver' has, happily, never been moved and stands at what was once the junction of Union Street - Bank Of England Place, here seen running down behind the clock tower and George Street, running left to right across this view and Lockyer Street, from where both pictures were taken. The short but wide flight of steps to the left are those of the old Theatre Royal Hotel, a building which, like so much of the rest of this early view, was destroyed during the Blitz. The old Theatre Royal itself was pulled down just before the war (1937), while the current building to bear that name, and which dominates this view, was opened in 1982.
EH 05 May 1998

ST CATHERINE'S CHURCH   Another Blitz
survivor, St Catherine's Church was built as a Chapel of Ease for St Andrew's in the early 1820s and opened on October 4, 1823 by its first vicar Robert Lampen. The building was another of Foulston's efforts and added to his already substantial contribution to this area which had been, until 1810, outside the main development of Plymouth. The Athenaeum, Theatre Royal and Royal Hotel (which stood opposite this church) were Foultson's earlier achievements here. Many Plymouth couples, still around today, were married here as it remained open until December 1957, just a few weeks after the restored mother church of St Andrew's had been reopened. Demolished soon afterwards, the entrance to the car park at the rear of the council chambers now occupies the site. *EH 05 May 1998*

THE CIVIC CENTRE Formally handed over to the Corporation on 21 March 1962, Plymouth's new Council House was officially opened by Her Majesty the Queen that summer - on 26 July. Just over 200 feet tall and fully fourteen floors, it was the City's tallest building to date and was the source of much interest. Note how, in Roy Todd's Then photograph, you could almost be forgiven for thinking that this was the front and not the rear of the building. Now it has much more of a back end appearance.

BEDFORD STREET It was for something like Queen Victoria's Jubilee that someone had the bright idea of reconstructing a number of the old town gates, in wood and fabric, and at first glance they did look rather authentic. But look hard enough and you can see the creases in the cloth. The gate replicated is the old Frankfort Gate and, as we look at the old photograph, our vantage point is from pre-war Bedford Street looking towards the junction of Russell Street (to the right) and Frankfort Street (to the left). Oliver's Shoe Shop stood beyond the right-hand archway throughout the 1940s, prior to the reconstruction of the city centre. Our modern view shows us the same angle today, the 'gate' would have stood roughly where the tallest tree is now. *EH 05 May 1998*

ARMADA WAY To those who can remember it well enough, our Then picture looks quite recent. But a generation has been raised in the 25 years that have elapsed since it was taken. Dingles, too, has been raised by one storey, since the fire at the store. For the three happy young girls in our Now picture, Armada Way, has always looked like this. For them it is hard to imagine that the people sitting around tables, drinking coffee outside in the sun are on the site of what was once a busy route for cars in the city centre. For everyone else, it is increasingly difficult to imagine that 60 years ago this would have looked very different indeed. We would have been standing around the back of the shops that lined the eastern side of pre-war Russell Street, between Mill Street and Frankfort Square. *EH 05 May 2001*

ARMADA WAY Our then picture, captured by Roy Westlake, takes us back twenty years before the introduction of pedestrianisation and long before the construction of Sainsbury's, the Armada Centre and the Copthorne Hotel. On the skyline of both pictures though you can just about make out the top of the skyscraper at North Road Station – the white gable-ended building below it in the Then picture being the old Opporto public house. Clearly trees now obscure our view of the other side of Armada Way but above the old Cortina there we can see a green-liveried BRS Parcel Lorry and beyond that on the corner of Cornwall Street – Martin's Bank. Further left alongside Radio Rentals we can see Evans part of The Outsize Shops' chain. *EH 02 Dec 2000*

ARMADA WAY With the recent chopping down of all the trees and shrubs in the lower section of Armada Way (between New George Street and Royal Parade), I suppose it's always possible that we may still see Armada Way like this again one day – although I don't think that the cars will ever be invited back. Main clues for dating our Then picture are the absence of the Civic Centre (therefore pre-1962) and the scaffolding around the Guildhall tower (during its restoration in 1958). *EH 24 April 2004*

SOUTH WESTERN HOTEL
One of the pre-war survivors in Plymouth city centre was the South Western Hotel, at the juction of York Street and Richmond Lane West. Built in the wake of the construction of North Road Station in 1877, it took its name from one of the companies which administered the new station, Great Western Railways and the London and South Western Railway. Photographed here in the early 1960s – there is still scaffolding on the almost-completed Civic Centre Building – it was demolished soon afterwards. Now the ramp up to the Mayflower Street car park occupies the site. For another bearing, look for the gap in the buildings lining the northern side of Cornwall Street in our Then picture. *EH 13 Nov 2001*

THE OPORTO One of the better-known, post-war landmarks to be cleared for the re-building of the city centre was the Oporto. Doubtless the reason for its fame was the fact that it managed to hang on so long, falling prey to the demolition men almost 25 years after the war had ended. June 1969 was the date of this sorry snap of the pub which for over a hundred years had stood at the top of York Street, a little down from, and almost opposite, the Albion and the Newtown. Today all those places have been consigned to the history books and the Copthorne Hotel stands proudly, it not a little bleakly, at the top of Armada Way. *EH 05 May 1998*

THE KOAN It stood just off Mayflower Street, in Armada Way, and at the time there were one or two other "works of art" dotted around, that were on loan to the City, There was another in the middle of North Cross Roundabout, although I can't quite remember what it looked like (a large packet of cigarettes comes to mind for some reason!). This though was The Koan and it was here in August 1972 when this photo was taken. A little later it simply disappeared. Imagine my surprise therefore, four years later when as a post-graduate student newly arrived at Warwick University I should see it again, this time outside the administration block of the campus. As far as I'm aware it's still there too! And I'm pretty sure it's the original and not a clone of the Koan. *EH 01Sept01*

108

YORK STREET Pictures of the long gone York Street are rare enough but to find one in colour as this wonderful Roy Todd shot was, is very unusual. It was taken originally from a point almost on the southern edge of North Cross roundabout – a little closer than our now photo suggests. The only contemporary features in our Then image are to be found below the skyline in the distance, all the other surviving post war features from the early sixties have gone. And as many will remember one of the last features to disappear from this view was the old Opporto The lone car driving up the hill incidentally is just passing the end of Oxford Place, part of which is now buried beneath Western Approach, and part of which still survives today.

MAYFLOWER STREET   At first glance there looks to be little difference, in the foreground at least but beyond the junction with Armada Way there is plenty to distinguish between these two images, which are separated by over 35 years. However as Mayflower Street still has regular vehicular traffic even the addition of the Armada Centre and the construction of the pedestrian bridge across to it from the car park does little to detract substantially from the similarities. Incidentally, it's remarkable to think that throughout all this time Jon Saberton has been keeping up with the fashions and keeping his customers up with them too in this particular stretch of the street. *EH 01 Feb 2003*

HARVEST HOME A true landmark of pre-war Plymouth, the much-loved Harvest Home was finally pulled down in November 1964 and here we see it about a year before the demolition men moved in. How long will it be now before the current generation of builders move in and raze this lot to the ground before starting all over again? For those who remember winding down around to the east of the Harvest Home, the long-gone Clarence Street and Park Street both ran off to your left as you made your way around the old Drake Circus into Old Town Street. *EH 30 Aug 2003*

CENTRAL HALL In 1817, the Ebenezer Methodist Chapel was built and in 1939 it was refashioned as the Central Methodist Hall. During World War Two and after the bombing of the Guildhall and Municipal Buildings, it was used for a number of civic occasions. In the Plan for Plymouth it was singled out, along with St Andrew's and Charles Church as being an important building to be preserved but 'in no way should it prevent the realization of the full scheme.' And so it has survived many changes since 1941, since 1966 (when our Then picture was taken) and will doubtless still be here in years to come when another shot from this angle will look very different again. *EH 06 Sept 2003*

SALTASH STREET The times they were a changing … It was the summer of 1965, in the pop charts Bob Dylan songs were enjoying great popularity and in Plymouth the new Drake Circus was appearing on the site of some of Plymouth's most impressive post-war survivors – the Old Tech, the Harvest Home and some of the centuries-old properties in Old Town Street and Saltash Street – you can see a fine example here, just in front of the then new Civic Centre. *EH 15 Nov 2003*

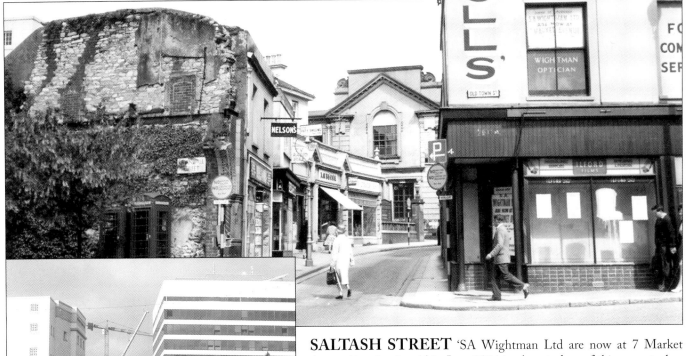

SALTASH STREET 'SA Wightman Ltd are now at 7 Market Avenue' is what it said in June 1964 in the window of this soon-to-be-demolished building. It stood on what was then the corner of Old Town Street and Saltash Street. The only visible key linking the two photos is the window of the Central Methodist Hall, seen in our Then view, just behind those buildings on the west side of Saltash Street. Forty years on this view is about to change again, although that window and the building that houses it, is not yet under threat. *EH 28 Feb 2004*

ROWE STREET The few words on the back of Frank Osborne's atmospheric snap from 1963 state simply that this is "Cobourg Street, taken from Tavistock Road … from outside the Harvest Home." Today the only element common to both views, however, is the unassuming little street that runs across the middle of this scene – Rowe Street – seen here in our Then picture behind the long-familiar advertising hoardings. There must have been a general election imminent, note also the ads for Sellecks, Paignton Zoo and Players cigarettes. A fascinating aspect of this forty-year-old photo though, is that at that time Allen's Garage hadn't been built then and now it's gone, although latterly it was Le Kepi Blanc and before that, the Chicago Rock Café. *EH 11 Jan 2003*

DUKE STREET Duke Street was a short stretch that ran between Saltash Street and the top of Old Town Street, bottom of Tavistock Road, with Clarence Street on the other side of the junction – beyond the building with the OXO sign. Today the line of the front elevation of those south-side Duke Street properties is a few metres in front of, but roughly parallel with, the uninspiring back line of the now-doomed early 1970s back line of the Drake Circus complex. Let's hope that what replaces it looks more attractive from this angle. *EH 07 June 2003*

DRAKE CIRCUS It's a view that many older Plymothians will readily recall but will be probably pose a bit of puzzle to the younger generations. The obvious key that links the two is the Civic Centre, and then, although it is obscured in our Now shot by the doomed 1970s Drake Circus block, the Burton Building provides a second contemporary visual fix. As the underpass is also scheduled to go in the redevelopment it will be interesting to see what this view looks like in a year or two. *EH 08 Nov 2003*

THE ROUNDABOUT A better Now vantage-point would have been from one of the empty office windows in that block (right of picture) which has been under threat of redevelopment for what seems like most of its thirty-odd-year existence. Here we are, on the fringe of the modern city centre, looking across to a location where the boundaries between pre- and post-war Plymouth begin to blur. Our Then picture has us looking up the top section of Old Town Street, a section which we can only relate to by focusing on the distinctive late-Victorian red-brick building located just below the library. Part of this was recently made into a multi-storey pub (Roundabout/It's A Scream) but this building is the only obvious link between the two images. *EH 08 Sept 2001*

BEDFORD VAULTS

It is difficult now to locate the vantage point which, until 1965, offered this view of the old Bedford Vaults. One of the oldest city-centre survivors when it was demolished. It stood in Old Town Street, between Saltash Street and Caxton Mews and it closed the year after this photograph was taken, in June 1964. *EH 20 Mar 2004*

POUND STREET It is hard, looking over this view today, to imagine a short street running up to the bottom of the library building at Drake Circus, with these buildings on either side. Many Plymothians recall walking along Pound Street, the Victorian Art School and Technical College off to one side, and the Harvest Home at the end of the block on their right. Many waited at bus stops where Western National, Royal Blue and Plymouth Corporation had pick-up points, as did Moorhaven and Moorfields hospital buses. *EH 08 March 2003*

DRAKE CIRCUS Bless the landscape gardeners for they, better than anyone, have an idea about how an area will look many years after it's been planted. Have a good look at our Then picture (taken by Roy Westlake), you know exactly where it is even though, as you can see from our Now photo, the scene has changed dramatically, in a vegetatious sort of way. Notwithstanding the advertising bollard – an imaginative use of old piping – the other changes here have been more subtle, most notably the cladding and signing of the building that was then Plymouth Polytechnic and is now the University of Plymouth. *EH 22 Jan 2002*

TAVISTOCK ROAD Prince and Butler (Men's and Boy's Outfitters), Cox and Lockyer, The Television Theatre, Dawson's Butchers and Thompson's stationers, those were the main businesses in that short stretch of Tavistock Road, between the Revenue and the Harvest Home, just before the demolition of these properties in the mid-sxities. Just up from them we see the equally-doomed old Tech building and behind it the then new Technical College that is now part of the University of Plymouth. So much change in such a short time and still plenty more to come. *EH 22 Nov 2003*

SHERWELL CHURCH This was the view exactly thirty years ago from outside the Harvest Home, at that time the pub had about a year to go, while the old Technical College dominating this view on the left had another three years before it would be razed to the ground – it had been there over sixty years. The oldest major building still standing in this view, the Sherwell Church building, is now part of the University and it could be that before too long the Museum, Art Gallery and City Library could also become University departments, meanwhile it's quite possible that years from now the first of these structures to give way to fresh development will be the University's main block itself. *EH 23 Aug 2003*

PUBLIC SCHOOLS Who could possibly have predicted the changes that have taken place here in the past forty years – or the changes still to happen in the next ten? Here we are in 1965. The old 'Tech' had just been pulled down, the new tech is not yet a polytechnic and a long way off becoming a university. Public Schools for girls and boys are still both thriving, while across the road Cobourg Street has yet to see the construction of the Allens Garage building, which would become a pub and which has just been demolished. *EH 09 Aug 2003*

HARVEST HOME The main building in the middle of the old picture here stands on the corner of Portland Place East (now Portland Close) and Tavistock Road and occupies the site now taken by the University main hall. Long before the University, though, came the College Of Technology. In 1967 the eight-storey block, since extended, opened not long after this picture was taken. Less than three years later the College had been restyled Plymouth Polytechnic and more recently has come the transformation into the University of Plymouth. Visible in both pictures is the Civic Centre and our second shot reveals just where the old Harvest Home stood in relation to the present Drake Circus roundabout.

120

TAVISTOCK ROAD AND CITY MUSEUM If Tavistock Road looks than much narrower now than it did forty years ago then try to imagine it one hundred years ago. Then the buildings on the eastern (Museum) side of the street ran along the line now represented by the broken white line down the middle of the road on that side of the barrier. Note, too, how much wider the pavement is outside the Museum. It was around the time that the Museum was being built, 1907-10, that the east side of the road was cleared here and the present block on the Gibbon Lane corner erected. On the University side of the road the buildings we see here in the old picture, including the long-remembered, yet temporary, post-war Nissen hut shops, were removed in the 1950s to make way for the widening of the road and the then new Technical College. *EH 05 May 1998*

121

PORTLAND PLACE Where now students stream from the main union building and library there would once only have been people living in and around Portland Square. Scene of one of the greatest civilian tragedies during World War Two the air raid shelter here took a direct hit during the Blitz and more than 70 people were killed. The area has greatly changed, as the university absorbs the sites around it. The Dartmoor Hotel, however, was long gone when World War Two started. Bought by members of Sherwell Church and demolished soon after 1899, it was long used as a car park for the church. Who would have thought 100 years ago that the church would be one day converted for use as a double lecture theatre for the University of Plymouth? Or that the congregation would find room enough in the adjoining church hall? *EH 08 Jan 2000*

SHERWELL CHURCH At first glance Sherwell Church looks much the same as it always has done, but look again at the roof and you will see a great skylight and below it a small dormer window. Internally the church has been impressively altered and is now part of Plymouth University, as indeed is the School of Maritime Studies, another comparatively recent building which can be seen rising up behind the back of the church. The Sherwell congregation, incidentally, still worship here, but not in the main building, rather in the former hall alongside, seen here to the right, just below the reservoir. Note the pair of policemen standing on the line of the present pavement and the pair of old phone boxes that stood where the traffic lights now are. *EH 05 May 1998*

DRAKE'S PLACE RESERVOIR The reservoir and the Church of Charles with St Matthias are the key features linking these two images, but look carefully and you will find the Stratton Creber Building, at the entrance to Armada Street on the far right of both pictures and many other properties, notably Bedford Terrace, little changed in between. The biggest changes are perhaps in the reservoir itself, unused and looking very sad and neglected these days, and the large building just to the right of the fountain on the left – this is now the site of the RAOB (Royal Antidiluvian Order Of Buffaloes) Club. *EH 05 May 1998*

ST LUKE'S While the view looking up Tavistock Place hasn't changed all that greatly in the past fifty years, if you were to have been leaning on that lamp-post looking south when our Then picture was taken, you would have seen a vastly different vista. No Art College then at the end of Regent Street, as the short kink in the road led us down towards Drake Circus. Back then, St Luke's was still a church, indeed after the wartime destruction of Charles Church, this was, for a time, in the 1950s and early 1960s, the parish church of Charles with St Luke. Then it was superceded by a new arrangement with St Matthias and the library services took over the building. In this now student-dominated environment, neighbouring properties have found favour as cafes. *EH 18 Jan 2003*

ART COLLEGE And still the building work goes on around here, but what subtle changes can you see around the Plymouth College of Art and Design, in our Then picture, not long after it was officially opened in March 1974. Clearly the trees have grown in the intervening years, so too has the amount of signage, on and off the building itself, and the height of the barrier down the middle of this busy thoroughfare. The other buildings look much the same from this angle but their usage, thanks indirectly to the increased number of students of both here at the Art College, and across the road at the University, has changed dramatically - especially the old school of motoring building (now a pub) and Sherwell Church (now lecture theatres), the spire of which we can just see behind the former St Luke's Chapel. *EH 19 Feb 2002*

EASTLAKE STREET Our Now picture sees us standing much closer to the end of the street than Roy Todd was standing when he took the earlier shot, forty years ago. What is the street? Then, it was Ebrington Street, but since then the construction of Charles Cross car park and since the dual carriageway (Charles Street) from Drake Circus to Charles Cross Roundabout has cut through it, the western section of this thoroughfare has been renamed Eastlake Street. The clear key linking both images is the Marks and Spencers building at the top of Old Town Street, running at right angles to our view. None of the buildings on the right, from the Ham Street Vaults down to the end, were left after the redevelopment, but on the southern, left-hand side there are a number of notable survivors. *EH 07 April 2001*

MARKS AND SPENCERS It is hard to believe that more than 50 years separate these two images and harder still to imagine what this same view will look like in five years time. Elements of old Plymouth survived in Drake Circus well into the 1960s, but now some of those changes are due for an early page in the pictorial history books. The steelwork is for the Burton building - Marks & Spencer had only just opened. *EH 31 Jan 2004*

EASTLAKE WALK A lone tram trundles along Ebrington Street towards a largely traffic free junction, where old Old Town Street splits into three, south, north-east, and north-west, as it bends around either side of the old Drake Circus. Today the curvature of the Burton building helps us plot the similarity between the two views, although the modern building is a metre or two to the west of its pre-war counterpart. For fifty metres or so, the line of this part of Ebrington Street is much the same, except that this section is no longer known by that name, having been re-christened Eastlake Walk in the redevelopment. A number of pre-war buildings survive on the southern side of the street here and a good many more can be found in the other "half" of Ebrington Street on the other side of Charles Cross car park and roundabout. Meanwhile, on the other side of the road, while the future of the present day Drake Circus development still hangs in the long term balance the Foto First shop now occupies that part of the old Drake Circus immediately to our left in the Then picture (many will recall the Guinness Clock that sat at the top of this block). This in turn places the site of the old Ebrington House building just across from the taxi rank outisde Burtons. *EH 03 April 1999*

DRAKE CIRCUS There were major changes to this junction back in the 1890s; Old Town Street was widened, buildings were demolished and indeed I've found photographs from that time filed under "Plymouth Blitz" before now. At the beginning of the twentieth century our Then picture was taken. Clearly there was a lot of devastation here during the Blitz and Old Town Street was refashioned again, over a period of twenty years or more. Now, just over thirty years since the completion of the modern Drake Circus, everything is up in the air – or rather down on the ground – again and you can but wonder how long it will be, if ever, before the entrance to Ebrington Street looks remotely like this again. *EH 19 June 2004*

GUINNESS CLOCK It is hard to believe that this view is destined for major changes in the near future, particularly when this photograph was taken less than forty years ago, in July 1965, just before the old Drake Circus development was demolished. Clearly, our Now picture is going to make a good Then one soon and in another forty years… who knows? Incidentally, although that red-brick block was well-known for housing the celebrated pre-war Guinness Clock and its attendant flashing signs, the advertising in question only appeared in 1937, just a year or two before the outbreak of hostilities. *EH 16 Aug 2003*

BOOTS Boots new premises, opened in 1953, was indeed new when Roy Westlake took this snap for a local brochure, the caption on the back reads; "Modern styled buildings such as this are a feature of the City Centre", One might just as easily say today that the planting that we see in the Now picture is a feature of the City Centre today, as the pedestrianisation planting of the 1980s is maturing nicely. Interestingly enough, fifty years on, the Boots logo hasn't changed fundamentally, just in the way it's presented, meanwhile close inspection suggests that the New George Street sign is the original one. *EH 15 Feb 2003*

BOOTS The angle is about right, the elevation is a little out but the changes are fairly obvious. Here we are looking down the new Old Town Street in the early part of 1953, or perhaps very late 1952 – Boots' new post-war City Centre chemist's shop was opened in June 1953. The Norwich Union was already finished and Marks and Spencer had been trading here since 1951. Remarkably Boots and Marks are still here although there have been many other changes, including the pedestrianisation of what for many years after the war and certainly for hundreds of years before the war, was one of the city's busiest traffic routes. *EH 08 Feb 2003*

OLD TOWN STREET In 1804 a new market was opened behind the western side of Old Town Street and the inappropriately named East Street was cut through the bottom half of Old Town Street to meet up with it. Eight years later Drake Street was constructed at the top end of the street, thereby creating another access into the market. Before the war the market had been refashioned, somewhat, and today it is hard to image that this late-Victorian market scene, captured here in a quiet moment, occupied the site now taken by the car-park at the back of Lloyds Bank, between Royal Parade and New George Street. The particular view here being the back of the fast food outlet, which is now where the old East Street Gate to the market stood. *EH 05 May 1998*

CORNWALL STREET It's that non-pedestrainised, eastern stretch of Cornwall Street that we see here - consequently, at first glance, there seems to be very little difference between the two pictures. Look again however and there are a number of elements that have altered in the thirty plus years that separate the two images. Originally planned as the "food street" in the rebuilding of the city centre, already many food stores had been driven out by 1968 when our Then picture was taken but British Home Stores still had a food section and just this side of BHS there was a butchers shop - Dewhurst's. Meanwhile like that other major department store chain, Marks and Spencers, at the top end of the street, Halfords have been here since mid-1950s - the early days of the new Cornwall Street. However apart from the names above the shops all else suggests business as normal, although the parking meters here have been consigned to the history books. *EH 13 May 2000*

MAGNET RESTAURANT

The Magnet was one of Plymouth's best-loved restaurants for years and many a tear was shed when the Williams family and dear old Stafford decided to call it a day. Not only did the city lose a popular eatery but one of the more distinctive city centre frontages went with it. In its place is now a facade that you could find in any town or city almost anywhere in the country, or indeed in a number of other countries. Incidentally, can you see the old weighing machine outside the entrance - can't imagine many restaurants wanting one of them outside their premises today in this calorie-conscious world we live in now. As with the eating establishment there has been a name change nextdoor but the business is essentially the same, as, what was Curtess Shoes, is now Shoe Express. One door further along we see the old Millets premises before they moved into New George Street. No matter how hard you look at the photos though it's still strange to think that almost thirty years separates the two, the earlier shot having been taken in October 1970, some fourteen years before pedestrianisation was to change the external character of this part of Cornwall Street. *EH 22 May 1999*

MARKET WAY Thirty years separates these two images but at first glance, unless you've been down Market Way recently, you may be hard pressed to say which is Then and which is Now. The clothes, for once, do not give a lot away and even the recent cosmetic design work on the exteriors of the flats has decidedly late-sixties feel to it. As the brickwork work has been rendered over and the balconies above the Snack Box built out flush with the frontage, so there has been a tasteful improvement in the appearance of this and neighbouring blocks. As for the shops themselves, it's not quite all change as one of the City Centre's more enduring small stores, Radio Parts, has been trading here for many a year. The nature of the business has changed subtly over the years though, from the valve days when Mr Cook had the business, through Howard Frampton, who stocked both components and accessories, to the present day, under John Horton, where accessories and disco gear are the main line but specialist parts can still be obtained. Prior to the war, incidentally, Radio Parts had been based in Old Town Street. *EH 05 June 1999*

CORNWALL STREET Almost thirty years separate these two images – but despite the gap, the changes at the bottom end of Cornwall Street are less obvious than in other parts of the pedestrianised city centre. The market and the surrounding shops all appear much as they did back at the dawn of the 70s but in an ever-changing world, most of the shops have changed hands. Both butchers Bridgman and Beer – remember their sausages? have moved on and Uglows is now a name from Plymouth's baking past. Until last year Gryll's and Son was still a trading name in the market but last September it became Pepper's Deli, selling similar produce from the middle of the market. Note how the parking meters have been replaced by fine young trees. *EH 23 Jan 1999*

THE EAGLE Offering a clear view of the bottom of Tracey Street, this early, post-war picture of the end of Cornwall Street shows us that the pub, which has changed name almost every decade since it was built, was one of the last bits of the city centre jigsaw to go in here. Originally the Eagle, it later became Silks, then the Mall, the Pig and Truffle and is now… the Eagle again. Note Goodbody's on the corner of Frankfort Gate, and the sewing machine shop beyond the old, but then very new, Austin. *EH 15 May 2004*

PANNIER MARKET - OPENING DAY Forty years separate these two images of the Pannier Market and at first glance not much has altered. But look again, in the Then picture - originally a delightful colour photo, taken by Roy Todd, on opening day - we see the original lettering spelling out MARKET was white on blue. Now it is black on blue. Above the sign, the centre window has been whited out. The windows either side appear to be unchanged – but are they? Look again and you will see that each section now is made up of 32 individual panes, where before there were 50. In the foreground, too, there have been changes: Market Avenue is now more pedestrian-friendly. As well as the Zebra crossing, there is a circular pattern in the cobbles that has replaced the tarmac road surface and carried on over to the pavements. Otherwise, it's business as usual, except that most of the traders have moved on, as has the design of cars and vans. But aren't those old Bedfords wonderful – remember Matchbox produced a whole series of them with different advertising on the side? *EH 18 Sept 1999*

PANNIER MARKET One of the least-altered aspects of Plymouth city centre today – largely because it has so far avoided pedestrianisation – is the bottom of New George Street. Our pictures show it at the junction with Raleigh Street and looking down towards Market Way. Forty years ago, when the Pannier Market was newly opened, our Then picture shows that the southern side of Frankfort Gate was still under construction, as was the western side of Market Way itself. What has changed with the passage of time is the nature of the business conducted in this part of the city centre. Forty years ago you would have found a large number of butchers selling fresh farm produce and poultry. Now you are more likely to find fast-food outlets *EH 11 Dec 1999*

NEW GEORGE STREET ODEON When it opened, in time for Christmas 1931, the Regent (which later became the Odeon, as we see it here) could seat 3,250 and was one of the ten largest cinemas in Europe. Thanks to a combination of fate and fireproofing (involving what were then ultra-modern materials) the building survived the Blitz ten years later, and indeed, for another twenty years after that. Remarkably, it has now been gone forty years - ultimately a victim of the 1943 Plan For Plymouth. For those trying to picture exactly where it stood in relation to what is in this part of New George Street now, this wonderful image from the corner of Raleigh Street provides the answer. *EH 27 Dec 2001*

WOOLWORTHS People queued for hours to be among the first to shop in the first new store to open in the post-war City Centre – Woolworths - way back in 1950. Half a century on and fashions have changed and the frontage has too, but this well-used New George Street entrance remains recognisable nonetheless, some of today's electronic products would undoubtedly have bewildered those fifties shoppers. *EH 20 Dec 2003*

TOPSHOP The angle isn't quite right but it's not far off. Today, as we stand on the corner of New George Street and Armada Way, we are looking at the site formerly occupied by the Prince Of Wales, which originally was just along from the corner of what was then Frankfort Street and Russell Street. The pub was No 4 Russell Street and the queues here, which reach down almost as far as the Russell Arms, were assembled ready for the opening of Woolworths' new store, out of the picture to the left, in New George Street, in November 1950. *EH 28 June 2003*

NEW GEORGE STREET Apart from the cars, the planting and the fashions, this scene looks remarkably familiar to those who remember pre-pedestrianised Plymouth. But the changes are significant and if you look carefully at the Then image you will see that the bottom end of New George Street isn't even complete – the Pannier Market is yet to appear, as is Littlewoods. Roy Westlake's study of the street dates from sometime around the mid-to-late 1950s. Note that Stead and Simpson are sill in situ fifty years on, while WH Smith has moved down and across the street. *EH 24 Dec 2002*

LAWSONS Costers stood where WH Smith now is. Then, as now, Lawsons was next-door. Lawsons shop, in business since the beginning of this century, was rebuilt on virtually the same site as it had occupied before the war, while Costers was originally on the other side of the old Herald and Morning News offices. The temporary 'Shop at the Co-op' building stands on part of Courtenay Street but the Co-op still occupies most of the site to our right, down as far as Raleigh Street. Note also the removal of cars and parking meters now in New George Street. Visible too is the post-fire extension, upwards, of the Dingles building; otherwise, apart from the pedestrianisation, the only major difference is alongside the old SWEB building. *EH 05 May 1998*

WESTERN MORNING NEWS AND EVENING HERALD There are few traces of pre-war Plymouth in the modern City Centre, and this façade is a tenuous and not particularly deep-rooted one. Tenuous because, since the Western Morning News and Evening Herald moved their base from here to Derriford in 1993, there is only the front wall left from that time. And not deep-rooted because the premises only just qualified as pre-war, having been opened on December 1, 1938, less than a year before war was declared. Back then this was Frankfort Street, with the imposing late Victorian Co-op below it. Today it is part of New George Street and has the new Co-op Derrys department store, just a little further to the west. *EH 05 Nov 2002*

LEICESTER HARMSWORTH HO.

Although the building behind has gone and what remains is literally just the facade, at least it serves as a lone token of pre-war Plymouth (and an original street line), inside the main city centre development. It is, however, only just pre-war, having been opened, as Leicester Harmsworth House, on December 1 1938. The extension on the right, incidentally, which picks up the modern street line, was added after the war. *EH 05 July 2003*

FRANKFORT STREET A lone City Centre survivor of the Blitz today, the front of Leicester Harmsworth House, marks the line of the old Frankfort Street, now re-aligned and renamed New George Street. The original building was named, on its opening, by Leicester Harmsworth's son Sir Harold Harmsworth, almost a year after his father's death. In the mid-1990s, the old building was removed and today only the front wall and roof remain. In the wartime picture we see that part of the pre-war Co-op which survived the bombing, but not the post-war re-planning. *EH 05 May 1998*

UNION STREET/DERRY'S CROSS The gas logo has long gone from Radiant House and there are other changes within this stretch of Union Street. Essentially, though, apart from the growth in the middle of Derry's Cross roundabout, the changes here over the last 40 years have been slight, certainly by comparison with the changes since the late nineteenth-century view of the same piece of Plymouth. It's hard now to imagine certain parts of old Union Street, particularly on this side of Armada Way – from the erstwhile Odeon (currently the Millennium) down to the Palace. The old street is more familiar. But there was no Odeon cinema (originally the Gaumont) when our Then shot was taken. *EH 09 April 2002*

UNION STREET The topography and the Union Street street-line line-up particularly well. However, I'm sure that if the chap in the bottom right hand corner could have been transported in time from then to now, he would not only marvel at what he saw, but he would also, doubtless, have difficulty believing that he was standing in the same spot as before. That's especially the case as the tram lines in front of him and the train lines that ran above and behind our vantage point are long gone. *EH 05 June 2004*

POST OFFICE UNION STREET Our Then picture takes us back to the early '50s. The Prince Regent has yet to be built to the left, on the corner of Western Approach, and there is a gap before the next building on the right, here in the eastern stretch of Union Street. Purpose-built as a Post Office, it has been a good few years since it operated as such, and with other buildings in this part of town recently, currently or imminently undergoing radical transformations - the casinos, Koolarus and the old Drake Cinema - it will be interesting to revisit soon for another Then & Now. *EH 23 April 2002*

DERRY'S CROSS Looking at the street scene surrounding the guy in the foreground, our Then picture from 1964 contains many changes, most of which need no pointing out. The construction of the Theatre Royal on the eastern side of Derry's Cross roundabout is the most obvious, along with the disappearance of the earlier buildings there. Then there is the disappearance of the Lockyer Tavern and the change in ownership of the various businesses here. One, though, Sparrow's newsagents, here on our left, just beyond what was Toy's Chemist Shop – is still going strong 40 years on. Look out, too, for the changing street furniture – do you remember the concrete bins and outdoor weighing machines? *EH 11 June 2002*

UNION STREET RAILWAY BRIDGE The original bridge was widened more than once, as the rail traffic in and out of Millbay Station increased between 1850 and 1940. After that, it went into decline and in the 1960s the station closed altogether, with the bridge finally coming down in 1974. With the opening of the Pavilions in 1991, Union Street was once again bridged in much the same place although not in the same way. This stretch of the strip looks vastly different today, at least at first glance. Look again, though, and you will see that the buildings beyond the bridges look much the same now as they did 100 years ago. They have changed little since the first were built in the 1820s. *EH 02 July 2002*

UNION ROOMS It is curious that although the building lines are similar and the vantage point is the same, there are absolutely no elements that are physically common to both pictures. Everything we can see in our 1950s picture is long gone; the bus station, the Wellington, the railway bridge over the top end of Union Street. In their places are the Pavilions, the Union Rooms and the pedestrian footbridge from the Pavilions to the Western Approach car park. *EH 10 Sept 2002*

UNION STREET/GAUMONT What great changes there are between these two images, separated by 53 years. Throughout that time, however, the old Gaumont building – now the Millennium nightclub complex – has changed little from the outside. Inside, the changes have been enormous, and after 32 years as a cinema, in 1963, part of it was converted by the Top Rank group into a dancehall, the Majestic Ballroom. In 1980 the part that had become the Odeon luxury cinema was also closed and refashioned, briefly as a rollerina and then as a nightclub. Then they were separate; since 1999 they have been interlinked. Everything this side of the bridge, of course, has changed out of all recognition, the bridge itself being one of the last pre-war elements to disappear, in 1973. Strangely, though, the pedestrian bridge linking the Pavilions with the Western Approach car park has a very similar effect from this angle and provides excellent photo opportunities for Then and Now comparisons, as the old railway bridge was a regular favourite with the early photographers. *EH 29 July 2000*

THE BALLARD INSTITUTE FOR BOYS

BALLARD INSTITUTE Come on then, Ballard Boys – doesn't this take you back? Remember the marvellous building, the fun on the roof and the rinkeries there on the left, just out of the picture? This was, and sill is, a busy corner on the edge of Millbay and the Ballard Institute was, for a decade or so, until it was bombed in the Blitz, a very popular recreation centre for hundreds of Plymouth boys. After the war, of course, Archie Ballard's generosity was perpetuated in the building of the modern-day Ballard Centre off the Crescent, but for many years this particular corner was left untouched. Until, that was, Telecom House was constructed here, with its fine view out to sea and across Millbay into Cornwall. Curiously, in more recent years, the building has become the offices of a firm that was formerly based in the Crescent – the large legal practice of Bond Pearce. Clearly, apart from the old walls and the fringes of Millbay Park, there is little to link the two images, but look carefully and you will see that the four trees are the same ones that appear in the earlier shot – over forty years on. *EH 08 April 2000*

MILLBAY BARRACKS Tuesday October 20, 1908 is the date on one of the posters on the wall outside the old Millbay Barracks and, over those ninety years, what a lot of changes you would have seen, standing on this corner. Archie Ballard would have known this view well from the twenties through to the Blitz when his great Institute stood just out of picture to the left, where Ballard House (formerly Telecom House) now stands. Incidentally, close examination of the old posters reveals that Argyle were at home to Brentford in the Southern League and Albion were at home to Plymouth! Less distinct, but just visible on the 1908 print of this corner of West Hoe Road, is the spire of Plymouth Cathedral, the one element, apart from the stonework and road layout, that links the two images. *EH 05 May 1998*

UNION STREET Union Street was laid down in the 1820s, but before then, King Street was the main route out of Plymouth to Stonehouse and Dock – Devonport. But here is Union Street in the early 1900s, showing the No 5 tram which ran along this route between 1898 and 1924. The old picture is taken looking towards the city centre from the railway bridge to Millbay – which was roughly where the present footbridge is between the Pavilions and the Western Approach car park. Victorian Union Street was a mix of shops, hotels and restaurants. This end of the famous street, today, is intersected by the complex traffic routes which take motorists north, south, east and west of the city. *EH 15Sept 1997*